Nights of
Whiskey and Roses

Nights of Whiskey and Roses

Volume II—Chicago by Night

Mark40e

iUniverse

NIGHTS OF WHISKEY AND ROSES
VOLUME II—CHICAGO BY NIGHT

iUniverse books may be ordered through booksellers or by contacting:

iUniverse
1663 Liberty Drive
Bloomington, IN 47403
www.iuniverse.com
844-349-9409

ISBN: 978-1-5320-5057-2 (sc)
ISBN: 978-1-5320-5059-6 (hc)
ISBN: 978-1-5320-5058-9 (e)

Print information available on the last page.

iUniverse rev. date: 10/19/2020

Contents

When I was growing up, I had this old TV set – a Panasonic of some sort with no remote control. 30 inches across…maybe bigger. One of the knobs broke at some point and I would use a spoon to turn the dial and change the channel. Eventually I threw that TV out and picked up a new one - and I've had it ever since.

I'm not sure what this has to do with anything, but for some odd reason it's the first thought that came to mind as I sat down this evening.

It's funny. The random thoughts that spring up as the day progresses. We think of old friends, new problems, bills to pay, and even old TV sets gone to waste.

So with that in mind, I realize I have more to ponder. More to write. More to photograph. More to live.

Dear people, let me tell you: if we love each other enough to kiss and make up, we're going to make it. And if we hate each other enough to care, there's still hope.

At one point in my life, I vowed to fuck every girl I wanted to fuck. And I was pretty damn successful, if I say so myself. It was like magic, walking in to any bar in town and picking the one with the longest legs and biggest smile. Full breasted blonde sex-kittens looking for a fix.

Eventually though, I grew tired of the grind. I got tired of handing them back to the world for consumption, as they tried desperately to hang on. I was vicious. And it wasn't pretty. In time, it was really quite ugly…

So now, I'm all better…feel great – ha ha.

And I'm happy to report from my new vantage point that we're going to make it. All of us. Even if, at times, it feels like we never will.

Just breathing is proof we've still got a fighting, hating, and loving chance.

Use it wisely.

++

Some of this is for Julie. Whose desperate phone call in the middle of the night hardly made a difference...

But eventually,
it did.

clark street at diversey; chicago

Let's Begin

i never solved any problems when i was angry. in fact i never met anyone who ever did. so with that in mind
i offer some free advice as we begin:
when someone tells you "don't worry", that generally means that THEY are not too worried.

But don't be fooled. Worry (without letting it consume you).

if you love, do it with all you've got. but if you don't have love, don't bother looking for it. chances are pretty damn good that it's coming straight at you in the body of someone searching harder than you.

patience…

lastly: good to remember that one man's trash is another man's treasure. this goes for old cars, old dishes, old clothes,

and women. too.

these are things to consider when staring in to the eyes of that character in the mirror every night.

getting it right now and then is a beautiful thing. but getting it wrong adds up too. so keep it up. good or bad. beautiful or bleak.

keep on keepin' on…no matter
everything you've ever done, hoped for, or discarded.

and keep in mind that with all that you are, look around you because

THIS IS IT.

just keep on loving whether you've got it or not.

the morning after; chicago

These Are City Stories

...and it's in the chicago morning
that everything gets sorted out best.

although i've mostly lived for the nights,
it's the next day that i love so much.

when you wake up next to someone beautiful
you've never known,

the possibilities
are

endless...

December Resolve

...and the cats have taken their place on the bed.

the sound of the rain drops tick,
sizzle and tumble down my window.

somewhere there are a million flowers blooming.

but
not here.

not in Chicago (in the middle of december).

here in chicago, there are only rain drops and cool northern winds
hinting of the snows to come.

soon the snow will blanket the city in all its white glory,
giving way to the gray mud and slush of februarys past
and
to come.

ahhhhhhh,

but summer.

summer may be months away
but
the thought of it makes me smile...

i'll make my way to the bed.

i'll try to get some sleep.

ferry to koh phagnan, thailand

On The Ferry Boat to Koh Phagnan Thailand (quick trip to asia)

with each ferry i have found myself
further and further from civilization,

yet
i feel a closeness to myself
unattained
in recent paths.

i lay on the beaches of koh phagnan, thailand...

the hippies
the ravers
the endless girls of this endless summer.

the beach is alive
with
combers and sleepers alike.

music drifts.

clouds lay like an array
of silk table clothes
over
the surrounding mountains.

fishing boats drift away
from the shore each morning,

and
the ferries bring hundreds of
wanderers at at time,
all searching...

the tan girls of israel bounce and smile.
they ask,
"where are you from?"
"chicago",
i say.
and they tell me stories of funny scottish men,
imitating their accents true.

i am a novelty among novelties,

and
thoughts are so easy to come by

a message comes
from 7000 miles away.

the girl says that
she is taking herself
off of my list.

(can't she understand?)

i sleep until it is no longer needed.

i eat until i can eat no more.

i love until there is nothing left to be said.

and still,

in a million rooms,
lovers lie in waiting

or in wait.

self portrait

CUSP

i have always found myself on the cusp
of a thing unseen.

thick
and
unforgiving,
it has always embraced me

and held me
in its selfish way.

ils regardante ce que je regarde.
mais ils ne voient
pas ce que je vois...

good night.

The One For The Moment

she spreads herself
across the bed
and
pulls the covers to her chin.

i can sense her content
yet
i know
that
she is still lonely.

she yawns and scratches her cheek.

...i know that we will soon
be asleep.

outside,
the sounds of the city buzz...and the streets below
rumble with the chatter of the neighborhood.

outside my window,
the winds
carry their fate...

sweet girl,
we have been delivered
from ravage and aloneness

if only for the moment.

good night sweet girl...good night.

see you in the morning...

Drops of Rain Water Falling Against The Window

april 21st
and drops of rain water are falling against my window.

it is a quiet time. only the
tap…tap…tap crackle sound of the rain.

the
way bacon sounds crackling on the stove
at age 9. seems like it's been raining for days.

a chicago taxi cab passes as i move toward the window...

the
afternoon is winding down
as
neighborhood people rush from the back seats of their cabs to the front steps of their buildings - trying desperately to dodge the tiny water drops falling from the sky.

the cat
leaps from his place on the chair and steps to the window to join me.

he
understands the rain

and
dislikes the crashes of thunder that periodically wake these tired walls.

but,

he is fascinated just the same
at
the drips of rain that weave through the screen...twisting and curling
their way down, forming a puddle at the base
before running off down the building face to the ground below.

i notice
the pretty girl from next door
as she steps from the back of her cab.

she
squints her eyes
and struts through the rain with
less fear than the others, heels clicking.

the
phone rings...it is tess,

and she's chattering at the other end of the line
about
how her work day was...

the afternoon news is playing on the television now. and tess, well,

she never stops.

as she talks and chatters, i watch the
water continue to
fall against my window.

the cat returns to his place on the chair

and
i wonder
just how long
the
rain
is going to last.

Space Girl

you fly around the places of my mind
and tempt me with those sad, red lips.

i can only imagine the way
my fingers would feel
if you were lying here now,
in this room with red walls
and sleeping cats.

Space Girl

you'll come to me wrapped
in a blanket of nighttime stars.

the colors of the sky will spin
and drip in to my room.

in the late afternoon
we'll lie entwined.

and in a million rooms
no one will know
the scents and sounds of our moment.

Space Girl

won't you come down here and
stretch yourself across these white sheets…
while the colors of my soul
spin and drip
into you,

in the late afternoon.

chicago

In a World

in a world
of silver flickering rain

you stand with those never ending legs…something shocking and
lovely
in this place,
so dull and gray.

in a dream
of dark mystery

you slip in like a white cat…smooth and quiet.

in a life
of yellow pain

i fall in the gentle surrender of autumn leaves…

in a moment
of blue passion

i ache
for you to never end.

B
L
U
E

b
l
u
e

w
a
v
e
s

f
a
l
l
i
n
g

o
v
e
r

t
h
e

r
o
o
m

and settling in to the cracks...

fall to the floor
and try desperately to understand.

Reservations for Dinner

running late for dinner
i watch as she makes her way
back from the shower.

she walks across the room
naked
and bare foot
as
she dries her hair
with a blue towel.

for the moment,
her hair is brown.

she is so lovely.

with
those young breasts
and giraffe legs...a work of art from heaven.

like an angel
that has been
blown to me
through the winds of eternity.

i lay and watch her
from my place between the sheets.

i wait
in anticipation
for her to notice me.

she doesn't though.

she just steps to the mirror
in
slow motion
and
gently spreads
face cream
and eye liner
to
her angel face.

next,
she slowly spreads
lotion down her body,
over the shoulders,
arms
and breasts...down her legs,
bending
as she does so.

i feel warm
as she turns to notice me.

she says,
"get in the shower you lazy bum!"

i pull her to the bed
and she falls
over me.

i beg her for a kiss,
knowing full well that the dinner reservations
are waiting.

laying over me
she kisses me hard
as i grab her bare ass.

"i love you!"
she proclaims.

"mmmmmm - i love you too"
i say.

…and it is saturday night in chicago
as we kiss. then kiss again.

the city can wait a little longer.

Tuesday

sunny december day in chicago.

the yuppies are living the great american dream.

and i...

it is difficult to wake up on a tuesday
after drinking monday night.

and the sun burns my skin

so i hide under the covers and
wonder if i'll ever wake up.

tuesday is just another day

but today...no sirens,
no construction crews,
no birds...

the girl has been gone for a week
and
it is now just me in the silence of this room.

it is tuesday
and the rent is due…

She is So Sweet

in the moonlight at 3am.

she is so sweet
she is so sweet

in the moonlight
sleeping,
as i
resist it.

just
a few more moments
in my eyes
before
the sandman
works his magic
on me too.

ahh...
so sweet

she is so sweet in the moonlight.

here comes the sandman

she is so...
she is so...

here comes the sandman

she is so...
she is so lovely.

here comes the sandman

she is so lovely.

here comes the sandman

she is so sweet
in the moonlight.

she is so sweet

here comes the sandman

here comes...

she
is so...

London

For Jennifer

everything is everything at once.
there is no victory or defeat.

there are forks, and many roads...each with the same result.

observe
observe
observe

and remember what is ALREADY known.

or
walk
and watch.

walk
watch
learn.

at once,
you'll see all of the agendas,
concealed and obvious.

there are moments
that
will tell you

everything you need to know.

I Like to Watch You Sleep

i like to watch you sleep...

the sunlight through the window
against
your skin.

i like to watch you sleep

the
sound of your breathing
cuts
the silence.

i like to watch you sleep

here
in the late afternoon.

the hope
for you to awaken...

to watch you there.
sunlight through the window.

like a single white lilly
in
the valley of the sun.

every shadow,
curve,

and line,
enticing me deep inside.

you look just like a silent
and soft dream.

and my hungry lips…set to devour.

but suddenly,
i am gentle.

and i move to you,

unwrapping you. i hear your smile.

quietly now. and you breathe…eyes,
still closed.

LOVELY. is all i can think.

and isn't it…as we enter in to each other

like so many times
before…

A Letter After She Went Missing for Months

I always believed
if true love found you
and you lost it
it would be found again.

I always believed
words without sound would travel distances you
did not know.

I always believed
that in the darkest nights,
the traces of the truest love of your heart
would hear your sorrow
and hold you with comforting thoughts.

I always believed
you would never be far away,

and in a minute I would be
in your arms again.
from, Loree

Never Come Morning

i pray for the morning to never come.

i have walked to the other side of summer's edge
and
found only cool death
whispering in to the wind.

the moon strains against the dawn.

(surrender. it's the last thing we'll ever know)

blackness
screams silence
in to my ears,

my fingers
trembling.

pure gold dances down a rainbow's slope.
brilliant before a million eyes.

but on this morning
i
turn away. mostly in fear, or
mostly in sorrow.

never come morning
never come morning
never come morning

her yellow hair spills out
over
the blue sky,
but
it is something unseen that takes her away.

i am broken

stuggling against the cool winds
of winter…always sure to come.

Longest Moment

it was a moment
i could
hardly understand.

birds flew upside down
and
cows jumped over the moon.

snowflakes grew
on blue trees
and yellow
turned to red.

my mind racing over images of
school days gone by...

the wind
cast its shadow across an open road
as
i walked up a broken window
and
stared in to the sun.

raindrops wandered away.

a rainbow slipped between the sheets
and brought summertime to my spring.

i woke to a dream
of august time fireflies
and lazy cats
making their way to the water's edge.

the moon danced on the horizon
(or was it the sun?)

i closed my eyes to the
snowflakes making their way home...

Now

the past is mostly dead.

it is not neccesarily what has happened,
but rather
how we choose to remember it.

although it makes me smile now and then,
i leave the past where it cannot hinder,
or provide false hope.

WHERE - yes where,
is
the moment.

the present is everything we have.

in fact,
our future is dependent upon it.

like anything in nature,
let it flow in and around you...

allow yourself to breath it.

"i can no more hold the wind in my fist
or put fire to my chest without being burned."

i would not try to capture a waterfall
in a cup.

i can only make every day, my budding
and building
life.
every passing moment
is a chance
to make it better...

every passing moment
is a chance
to keep it that way…

New York

Abnormal

i met robert for a drink at 310pm.

that turned into to 3.

then,
a well done burger
at dublin's.

an irish spot in the neighborhood,
owned by a fat man,
not
from ireland.

ha ha…

so we downed 2 more
and
headed across the street to hunt club.

there,
we drank a few more.

"i like that one."
he said,
pointing to a the newest well breasted waitress…

i said,
"she lives in the neighborhood...i've seen her carrying her groceries
home from time to time."

he says,
"i'd like to carry her home right now."

"ha ha"
i replied.

i sipped my rolling rock.
(a rare occurance,
since i generally stick to jack and coke)

but
it is tuesday.
and for the first time in a LONG time,
chicago has passed 75 degrees. in honor of it,
i ordered a few beers.

(these are always long winters)

i said,
"that first time you see someone,
they always seem so larger than life."

robert didn't say anything
but
i know he knew.

after a long pause
he says,
"you are too analytical. lighten up and enjoy the scenery."

i said,
"normal people don't do this shit."

he said,
"what are you talking about, man?"

we watched the well breasted waitress do her thing for another hour
or so,
drank a couple more,

and i said,
"i'm going home...i have something to do."

tuesday night.

i stopped off at potash market to buy a few bottles of wine and started
in to writing upon returning home.

"every day people" never do this.
abnormal is nice...really nice.
abnormal means drinking on a tuesday afternoon
and staring at lovely breasts before ending the night. abnormal means
thinking only *you* make sense
even if you question it now and then...

955pm now
and
i'm still tapping at the keys

a fish
in all of its' beauty
cannot fly.

jessica calls. she is on her way over. bringing her long
legs and insanity.

abnormal
means taking that call and showering
before the night gets even better yet…

amsterdam

Out of Chaos

out of chaos
comes simplicity.

it exists there,
in the middle of the dance.

Monday April 7ᵀʰ

and once again
the chicago sky
has seen fit to dump a significant amount of snow
to the ground…here in the early spring.

i stand at my window,
18 floors above oak street
and
fix my eyes on the horizon...

(where is the sun?

where is the sun?

where is the sun?)

eventually i make my way to the kitchen for a glass of milk.

i won't
be going
outside today.

35

she asked,
how long have you been 35 years old?

i said,
i don't think
i'll ever be 35...
or
any age...i just exist.

she said,
you seem like one of those characters that has always been the same
age...all those opinions and judgments of the world around you are
firmly in place.

i said,
i don't judge the world around me the way you may think...i only
make a judgment determining what is good or bad for me...feels good
and i go with it...feels bad and i turn away from it...very simple.

in that sense, nothing is ever truly bad or truly good...only bad or
good for the individual experiencing it.

what works for another may not work for me...something you can
surely understand.

NO!
she said
you are too close minded.

i said,
i just love it when people say
'you need to have an open mind and be less opinionated'
when what they are really saying is,
'you need to agree with me'

i say: keep your opinions and i'll keep mine...if they coincide now
and then, then let's drink over it and compare notes. should we
disagree now and then, let's have a clean, spirited debate over it and
laugh over our differences, appreciating what each other bring to the
relationship.
she said,

i NEVER judge others.

i said,
didn't you just make a judgment about my 'being one of those
characters that always seems to have been the same age...opinions
and judgments firmly in place'?

if it is not a 'judgment', it certainly is an opinion...no?

she said,
you are SO arrogant.

i fucked her. hard.

then i rode the bus home and walked over to the coffee shop...

another relationship
down the drain...

but it was…something

while it lasted (a few days or so?)

i can't remember.

ha ha ha…

From One Red Room to Mine
(gato de la noche)

william stopped by
around 1030pm...2 bottles of wine to match the 2 i had in my fridge.

we're going out tonight
he said.

ha ha,

i said,
not me, man...i'm in writing tonight...and listening to music. this is
MY night.

he pulled the cork off of the first bottle.

what for???
he asked,
handing me a glass, telling me it's SATURDAY and we need
to get out there...

we laughed and listened to music through 4 bottles of wine...3 white
and one red.

let's go on over to domaine,
he says. rush street looks good tonight.

he was looking out over the city
and down to the streets below.

i glanced at the clock...112am

they close at 2am, no?
i asked.

not sure,
he said.

we made our way out the door
and over to domaine. red walls and red wine colored drapery
everywhere...just in time for last call.

as we made our way across the red room, through the crowd,

she seemed to float in behind us.

badass boots, jeans, t-shirt and jean jacket. looking so...gato de la
noche. that was her.

she stood there.
10 ft away,
looking over the scene.

my guess?
5'7"
108lbs
american...but foreign born parents.

boyfriend problems for sure.

she worked her way to the bar...

how about a drink?
i said, smiling...
you look like you may need one.

49

she smiled,
put her arm around my neck
and said,
you think so, eh?

what'll it be,
i asked

beer,
she said.

beer?
beer? what does a girl like you want with a beer?

i like it,
she said.

i ordered her an amstel,
jack and coke for me, rolling rock for william...

the lights were coming up.

what has you out so late this night?
i asked,
handing her a cigarette.

where can we go?
she asked, suspiciously ingoring my question...

wonder bar,
i said.

we hustled over to wonder bar for a few drinks,

then eventually bought a bottle of wine from the bartender,
and made our way back to my place.

from one red room to mine.

once in the door
she says,
i like your red walls.

i said,
these are my two cats...this is my bed, and that's the bathroom
(pointing toward the bathroom door).

the results:
she is, in fact, 5'7"

american, with foreign born parents.
boyfriend problems. plenty. OH – and 105lbs (i was off by 3).

the next morning i said,
so what's next? you have to do something
about your man.

she said,
i have a lot of crap to deal with...i don't know.

she dressed,
a little less pep than 6 hours before...but we knew each other now.

interesting...interesting...these chance meetings.

i said,
hell,
i was having girlfriend problems of my own...so i can definitely
relate.

as she dressed i made a mental note of every inch and curve of her body.

beautiful. nearly brought me to tears...damn near brought me to tears.

but she already knew that - ha ha...she had me by both balls
AND my brains
upon entering that red room at domaine.

she comes by now, once or twice a week
to see my red room
and
sleeping cats. perhaps a bit more…because we devour
each other every time she walks through that door. all this,
despite our troubles.

and i smile every time she enters.

and william?

...well he got lost somewhere that night. i'm sure he'll come knocking
soon enough.

red rooms are waiting.

There Was A Time (my world)

there was a time
somewhere...i must've been
maybe 12
or 13. mom saw fit to leave me home alone
now and then.

"i'll be back in a couple of hours"
she'd say.

i'd look at the clock. it was always
around 2pm or so...dad was always home by 530 sharp
and i knew
that my mom would need about 45 minutes to
prepare dinner,
so i figured i had until at least 430 or so...

2 and
a half
hours to myself.

first
i'd pound the piano in the living room
making up frantic
cresendo'd songs
and naming them each:
haunted house
the gray ghost
haunted house II
sundays in october
the gray ghost II

53

etc, etc...i had this obsession with ghosts.

after a while
i'd be bored of that,
and build some sort of imaginary fortress
in the dining room.
turning the chairs upside down,
draping sheets and blankets over the top,
ducking from imaginary enemies
in an imagination filled afternoon.

330pm. another hour or so to myself.

i'd put the chairs back in order
and go digging through the garage.

sometimes i'd just lay on the couch in front of the TV and check my
watch,
waiting for the second hand to hit the 12.

shwoop!
i'd take in all of my breath
and time how long i could hold it...i'd see stars,
i'd see colors,
i'd see the faces of the cheering fans of my mind
as i went for the all time breath holding record...

4pm
where was my mom now?

i might then opt to arrange all of my micronauts and star wars
characters in a field of battle across
my bedroom floor.

they'd be standing there
facing off, ready for the battle of all battles.

i'd go for my camera and take pictures of them
making all sorts of explosion and laser beam sounds as i manuevered
them in to various stages of conquered territory.

430pm
and i'd hear the rumble of the garage door opening
as my mother returned.

"come help with the groceries!"
she'd shout from the distant side of the house.

i'd shuffle down the steps
and out in to the garage,
pulling plastic and paper bags,
peeking inside each one for
frosted flakes,

eggo waffles and
french fries,
never saying a word.

"thanks, son"
she'd say as i put the last bag on the counter top.

with that,
i'd run out the back door,
down the steps and in to the yard,
hop on my bike and pull a wheelie as i sped down the driveway...

"be back in an hour!"
she'd shout out the window,
"dinner is at 530 when your dad get's home!"

i'd race past mike wood's house
where his sister jennifer was usually
sitting on the front steps
crying because mike had hit her or called her some sort of name...

i'd pull another wheelie,
hoping
someone would take notice of my perfect form.

i always wanted people to admire me. i just didn't care much
for them talking to me.

i'd ride the neighborhood
till 520...

looking at my watch,
i'd pull a wheelie
and rip home.

upon arrival,
i'd race up the back steps, through the back door
to the scents of the early evening kitchen.

"wash up mister!"
i'd hear.

while washing my hands,
my father generally made his way through the door,
but i never heard him over the sound of the running water
(i learned the importance of timing
and watching your back over the years).

"hey kiddo - what've you been up to all day?"
he'd say...he always had a strange tone in his voice.

"nothing"
i'd say.

he'd chuckle in the adultlike manner i could never fully understand.

my world was my own,
and i was fully convinced adults
would never understand.

today…
i woke up late.

living alone in the middle of this city.

i rubbed my eyes,
admired the sleeping cats and
despised the red walls (my opinion of these red walls changes from
time to time).

i showered,
dressed,
and made my way outside.

once there,
i walked past various people of the neighborhood.

some i know,
some i just see over and over, but i never say hello.

sometimes they greet me and
i wonder
what they think of me. perhaps they're thinking the same…

i headed over to the coffee shop
and took my place over the daily Chicago Sun Times.

i laughed when i saw a real adult couple arguing over something one
said to the other last night at a dinner party among "friends".

and me?

the girl who was with me last night
left soon after waking. just in time for me to get back to my world.

i sat at the coffee shop for an hour or so,
then decided to hit the sidewalk again.

once outside, i took a deep breath
and headed over to the book store as the people just seemed to blend
together in strangeness…

i took the time to notice that my world is still good.

amanda; chicago

Sometimes

sometimes
a kiss is like magic. not always exactly what it seems.

sometimes,
things are exactly as they seem to be.

but
it doesn't last.

sometimes,
i wonder about that look in your eyes.

because magic or real,
i sense that it will never last.

sometimes,
you seem so cold.

sometimes,
i walk out in frustration - and you never come after me.

feeling foolish halfway up the block,
i turn around.

i come walking back in

to see you
lying on the bed.

On That Day

every once in a while i think about that day to come.

that time i'll be lying on a bed
a million miles from this page. my heart signaling to my body
that the ticks are winding down.

i'll be staring at the ceiling with eyes - the eyes
very much alive.

eyes
that will still be yearning to watch young girls,
sunsets,
or sleeping cats.

my fingers will be trembling as my
eyes move around the room for one last look
at the pictures next to the bed, the desk i sat at from time to time,
and wrote for so many years.
the garbage,
full of trash.
the door handle,
worn...

it will be a quiet time.

the bed beneath my aged back
and
my mind
full of memories both happy and sad.

i'll think to myself - i wish i had done this, or
i *should* have done that.

the photos,
love letters,
and stories
will be in the drawers,
waiting to be collected up and stored in the corner of
some distant relative's attic.

out in the neighborhood,
someone will be watering their lawn while on the radio
some new band is making its' run for the top of the charts.

in a million stores, a million people will be fumbling with dollars
and change
to pay for their trivial groceries and various items.

and me,
in this quiet room.

yes,
at that time,
any number of things will be happening in *this* world.

and me,
with a lifetime of memories...

when that day comes
i won't fight it.

when that moment arrives
i'll look over…

give the cats a wink
and drift off into that forever sleep.

i'll be closing my eyes to look for you in another place.

The

i know that i have always had plenty to say about true love
and all about it that can be glorious
                                        or false.

we all feel that we deserve
true love.

but
the sad truth is that no matter how much we feel we deserve something,

anything:
if it does not exist
we cannot have it.

SOMETIMES.

sometimes,
you meet
ONE.

one that makes your insides move
like earth tremors.

giant, gentle plates beneath
the earth.

a quake in your soul...

and
it's hard to let that one go.

from first glance,
you crave

the hair
the eyes
the lips

the neck
the shoulders
the breasts
the belly
the ass
the legs

the insides
the insides
the insides…

and
the gentle toes.

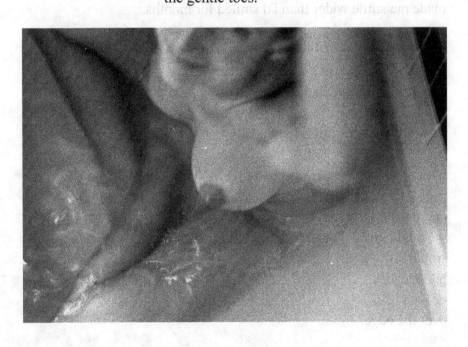

My Fingers Fumble Now

my fingers fumble now.

here in
the late of evening.

i reach for the milk,
knocking the cap to the ground
as
i wonder where you are...what you might be doing.

there were sweet nights
only days ago.

running in to you again
after all this time
made me smile wider than i'd smiled for months.

but of course,
like the last time we knew each other,
everything has fallen apart in a matter of moments.

we were always so tightly bound.

but everything was always hanging in the balance.

and the slightest hint that
we might end
would always
put one,
or both us
over the edge.

you said that you were returning to me this time,
a new person...apologizing for the agonies
of the first time around.

i've always said that a fish
cannot fly,

and
this time was no exception.

so within a matter of weeks,
here i am. alone again.

we're ex lovers again.

strange
strangers again.

and i am feeling quite strange
as
i sip my milk from the glass.

all the lovers in the world tonight,
could not soothe even one inch me.

my fingers are fumblng now

and suddenly i notice,

it is quiet...

        and 211am.

Recollections on A Monday Morning
(laughing any time i can)

the phone rings

841am...who the hell is calling me at this hour?

i check the caller ID:
jessica...the girl from last summer. it must be spring again if
she's calling (*wink*wink******haha*).

i don't pick up.
and decide to roll over for more,
much needed sleep.

my mind is on someone else now

and sleeping is my only escape from her

although
she manages to barge in to my dreams now and then.

girl.
where are you now?
and do you recall that first…
sitting at your place after a night of drinks at wonder bar...dancing
in the streets

and kissing as we waited for that magical cab to spin us home.

fuck.

do you recall the conversations
as i spilled red wine across your beige bedroom carpet?

ah yes,
that first night was a night of
whiskey and roses.

it wasn't long before we'd made
plans...(LOVE). the future
was looking good.

but that first road trip...ha ha. do you recall THAT disaster?
damn,
how do things get so fucked up.

i have this vivid recollection of our very last night. the one that ended
it all. for good.

do you recall the time between first meeting,
and
walking out the door for the last time?

do you recall falling in to that thing most people call love?

maybe that was the problem. ha ha...maybe. i always knew there was
no future in that witch's brew.

1012am now...the phone rings again...it's jacque. the best one for the
job these days...makes me forget. of course, i pick up.

"hey"
she says.

and for the moment
just the sound of her voice over the phone
makes me smile.

"what time are we going to the cubs game today?"

i smile
and say,
"not soon enough"

we agree to meet in a little while and
i stumble from the bed.

i recall that beautiful, magical curse of a girl who is so far away now,
and wonder about what might have been. but hell. jacque is next. and
if you saw her
you'd know that i couldn't ask for much more than that.

i just have to remember not to LOVE.

there's just no future for THAT kind of life...ha ha HA.

the warm, hot shower rains over me now.

There Was A Dr. In The House, But Fortunately There Was A Hair Dresser Too

the night started at home with
me pouring wine in to 2 glasses,
handing one to jacque
and handing one to myself (thank you, i thought).

she's all sorts of mixed up.
but the latina side emerges
after a few glasses - and as the music gets lively.

it wasn't long before she was dancing and bopping
around my place - her long hair flowing
and whipping as she spun. black.
like
a silky nighttime sky. and I mean that. really.

"let's go to puerto rico!"
she exclaimed.

"when?"
i asked.

"i don't know...let's just do it. maybe next month."

i contemplated this as we found our way out the door, down the
elevator, and in to the streets.

we walked over to wonder bar
and entered
around 1145pm - sunday night...

71

the place was jumping,
and lonnie was on the piano
at a jazzy-fever pitch...heather was on stage singing her heart out.

we made our way up to the bar and ordered drinks:
jack and coke for me. amstel for jacque.

well, this older white hair keeps eyeing her - and finally comes over
to introduce himself.
"I'M A DOCTOR"
he says.

he goes on to tell us how his wife recently left him "for someone with
more money," he explains...

it was quite a boring story,
but hey:
as he said,
he was a doctor.
and for him, that seemed to solve
at least a few of his troubles.

since i already have a doctor of my own,
i decided not to accept his business card
when he offered. i'm not sure if jacque has a doctor here in the city,
but for some reason she accepted the card with a smile.

she started to talk to me again,
telling me some story about...

then all of a sudden, someone yelled,
"DAMN! GIRL, YOUR HAIR'S ON FIRE!!!"

i noticed
a pretty damn huge flame almost beginning to engulf her head.

a few guys,
as well as me,
began beating at her hair to douse the flames...puff...puff...puff...and
the flames were soon killed.

the music stopped,
and heather,
from the stage, yells
"damn! what the fuck is on fire back there!!??"

the odor of hair and hair spray filled the air.

"you alright?"
i asked.
"i don't know."
she replied, a bit drunk and confused.

the doctor came scurrying back
and the other guys who helped out were waving the odor and smoke
away with their hands.

the doctor was examing her skin and neck
(putting his old doctor fingers all over her, naturally).

i wasn't sure if i should laugh,
but mostly i was in state of buzz and shock...

one of the other guys took the opportunity
to introduce himself,
"it's ok honey,
I'M A HAIRDRESSER!!"
he said.

he spent the next 60 minutes
fussing over her hair,

talking about the dangers of split ends
and the glories of a good conditioner.

i never quite knew that the answer to all of life's worries
resided in a good bottle of conditioner – but the hairdresser convinced
us all.

"you need to deep condition that when you get home honey!
...girl, i can fix this damage for you! i rememeber this one time when
this girl came to me that had gotten crazy glue in her hair!"

the doctor was throwing his 2 cents in now and then, talking about
the values of having a good doctor, etc etc....zzzzz...

everyone nodded in agreement over various points made...

i ordered another jack and coke and bought everyone a round of
shots...petrone tequila.

since i already have a barber, when the hairdresser offered,
i decided not to accept his card. and i'm not sure if jacque has a
hairdresser here in the city, but she accepted his card with a smile.

he went on to ask me if i might be interested in men,
to which i said,
"no."

and we agreed to do another round of shots.
which we did.

and everyone at wonderbar was feeling good again.

heather went on singing.

and it was good for all of us that
there was a doctor in the house...but thank god for that hair dresser too.

what a sunday night can bring to a person like me,
i rarely understand (you should try it some time).

it was about 230am.

jacque smiled, planted
a kiss on me,
and grabbed me by the crotch.

and wth that,

it was time to go.

somewhere in illinois

a short story, straight from the mind

The Quiet Lake

she says that no one ever wins in this town.
and i believe it
as the porch door swings shut.

we make our way
down the dirt road,
past the Gunderson house,
up the bike path
to the quiet lake's edge.

i strum my guitar as jenny strips down
and jumps in.

"HEY!"
she yells,
splashing water in my direction...
"C'MON IN!"

"not so loud!"
i yell,
noticing that i'm being just as loud as her,
"someone might hear!"

i sit here waiting for a moment
that i know i'll only come upon
from time to time.

jenny always tells me that i'm her hero...that
if it weren't for me, she'd burn every house
in town and ride away in mrs. robert's "old piece of shit."

"a car like that old piece of shit still has some life in it...it'll take you
anywhere at least once – and maybe twice," she sometimes says.

"C'MON!"
she yells.

and i love the way the sun
reflects off her blue eyes.

i know that all poor men in this world would much rather
be rich
or on their way there.

I also know that
all the rich men in this world could not buy happiness for all the
disappointed women...mothers and what not.

GOD GOD GOD
all these things in my head.

if i could just make this quiet lake the world,
me and jenny could just swim all day...then over to the shoreline to
cook burgers on a grill. lovely. so lovely...

THAT would be a painting that all the great ones across time would
call ART.

the smiles and the laughter would lift the colors off the canvas and
in to the laps of all
the critics...

and everyone would have cause to cheer.

(somebody say AMEN)

My Word Counts

i smiled
a soft smile...

laying behind her
                nibbling
                      at her ear as i held her in a tight embrace.

it was mid morning on a wednesday and niether of us had anywhere
to be.

she was looking for a specific response
when she asked me what it was that
i liked about her.

i didn't have the heart...no i didn't have the...

...let's just say:
it wasn't in me to tell her that
it was the special way she
bucked her hips...the curve of her ass...the breasts...the toes...or the
way it makes me feel, just to watch her walk in to my room.

the very thing she cultivated most
was the one thing she wanted me to
obsess over least.

like her sexuality...or her night moves.

well dear,
these are the traps only you could have set. something deep inside
you must've always known...

79

i am guilty of obsessing over you for your body and for your sex. and
if that is not enough,
well,

for the moment...for the moment,
it is going to have to be enough.

because enough or not...for the moment,
you have me...ALL if me. and my word counts.

let us have peace.

Can I Kiss You Once More

before sleep,
can i kiss you once more?

i lay here in the aftermath of a moment

                                        aching for your skin.

my body is weak
but
my heart is racing
like a wild horse.

can i kiss you once more before we sleep?

just once more
                 for luck.

i feel desperation
because
i know that you'll soon be a memory. (or was it a dream?)
destined to follow the same
drifting trail of the others.

just one more time...please just one more time.

i must kiss you
once more.

my angel...my angel...my angel

                         my sweet angel of the night...

V.

the phone rang. it was her. she said she'd be coming in to chicago for a few days.

a funeral.

what could i say? of course, i accepted the news with a smile.

and when she got here

i plunged right in.

things could be worse - ha ha ha...

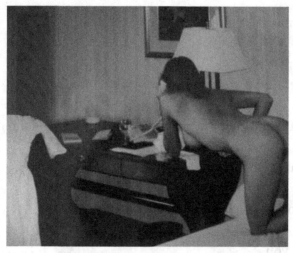

within minutes of her arrival; chicago

And Then There Was One

i could tear these clothes from your body
and devour you,
                        she said.

i could love you again,
                              he said.

i feel it again,
she said.

i feel it again,
he said.

afterwards
                    she said,
                          you are so quiet.

im only thinking,
he said.

and her tears flowed.

she looked in to his eyes
and said,
"we don't have to be this way...this doesn't have to be us."

and with that, he knew he would wake up alone again.

she left town the next day. an air plane lifting her to somewhere far.

and he sat quietly in his place...

i miss you,
               he said.

It Rises...It Falls

i have had the opportunity to
see things unseen.

i have tasted skin,
and felt my own **burn.**

i have been sober
when being drunk would have been better.

and
drunk
when sobriety was the only requirement.

i have distrusted my own emotion
when it would have been easier to love.

and she still has that look
in her eyes
when we meet in the darkness of night.

"i'm a lot like you",
she says.

"yes",
i think…

(I think we're the fucked up kind. dangerous to no one
but ourselves).

"i think you're right
sweet girl."

maple & state street; chicago

America's New War: On Bimbos

i think i'm declaring a new war: on bimbos

so
bimbos: unite

unite in your quest for pink phones, gold digging,
gossiping,
and selfish, catty-fake behavior...

pump up those breasts,
paint on that tank top,
and set your goals → low.

i see them more and more
now that the chicago weather has turned.

late morning, early afternoon
and into the night,

there they are. driving in from the suburbs
or catching taxi cabs on the corner of rush and oak.

sometimes they are weaving from an overdose of
mascara,
alcohol,
and bad pick up lines. sometimes
they are screeching in to their sparkly phones,
cigarette dangling,
and equally bimbonic friends bopping to the beat.

i have to laugh. because
taking it all so seriously would be a crime against
the soul. or worse yet,
a slap in the face of all things made of class – or dignity.

i wonder sometimes
what makes them go? is it the combination of caffeine,
tobacco,
and the hope for...wait.

what IS IT
they hope for?

in all my years,
i've never once heard a friend of mine say: "gee - tonight
i hope i meet some gold digging, pumped out bimbo
looking to spend my money...wouldn't that be nice? my mom
will love her, for sure."

never - ha ha...the thought makes me laugh even now.

but still,
they're out there,

as if
their high heels and fake, pink
nails matter. covering their faces with what amounts to
4 lbs of cake batter
and a half gallon of the latest perfume being promoted by MTV.

by 2am the mascara will be running down their cheeks as they
wonder
why the guy who bought them drinks at 11,
left with the bimbo
with the bigger boobs
and shorter skirt at 12.

"do you think i need a boob job?"
she'll cry to her friends...who will promptly respond,
"no way girl...you're PERFECT - that ASS HOLE just never saw it!"

"yeah",
she'll respond, "BITCH! that whore was a fucking slut, ANYWAYS!"

they'll all agree that the guy was a dick,
the girl is diseased,
and the next party will surely save them all.

i'm not sure if my war on bimbos will be such a good one. after all,
it's a losing one i suppose. these days they seem to be coming
at a faster and faster rate.

i've decided:
nice guys sometimes finish last,
but bimbos always manage to finish the job. and that vicious

cycle somehow has it's hypnotic allure. a formula for human disaster.

but i'm glad to be aware

and drifting away from that game. after all,
i wasn't always the nicest guy...but i never could stomach
a mascara dripping bimbo from the suburbs.

and although
i manage to keep from finishing last,
i'm surely,
surely,
surely, done with pumped up
mascara dripping bimbos.

so good luck bimbos of the world. you'll need it now
more than ever.

because the competition is fierce. and there is always
a bimbo willing to be more bimbonic than the one before her,

or the one who left with that ass-hole as the clock struck midnight.

When

when you look at a word long enough
it begins to take new shape,
almost

foreign.

it is the same way,
always,
              and with everything.

walking outside in the dead of chicago
winter winter winter.

after taking 20 or so steps,
running back to your door,
fumbling with the keys,
hands shivering,
teeth chattering,
heart pounding.

inside,
past your door man,
back to the elevator,
and
up up up to the 57th floor.

telling yourself that you are not
going anywhere today.

walking down the hallway
back to your door.

throwing leftover spaghetti in the microwave,
pulling a swig from the half gallon of milk,
miles davis on the radio.

no women...

but it is saturday. and knowing that they'll be out tonight certainly
sparks a spark.

3 days worth of dishes in the sink.
no children,

but 2 sleeping
gray cats

watching them sleep
as you suddenly become aware
of the quiet walls...so quiet today.

so foreign.

new orleans (photo courtesy of greg)

VI.

a kiss can save or enslave.

chicago

On Showering Afterwards

we often shower after our bodies have had their way.

and her face is always soft. peaceful. quiet. content.
we chatter a bit as the sounds of the water droplets
beat against the walls and floor. we know each other so well now
that everything just comes so natural.

she washes me from time to time,
spreading the soap over my shoulders
and down past my waist.

93

i look her over.

the belly
the back
the neck
the legs...the long long legs.

and i
grin
grin
grin as i wash her from
face to toe.

i lean against the back wall
as
she washes her own hair.

me, still grinning.

her eyes closed under the running water,
i take the opportunity to gaze.

                              lost...in bliss.

she spashes water to my face.

"what'r you looking at, you???"
she smiles and says.

feeling the good times. this tiny miracle of God called LOVE.

i kiss her once and step out. she often lingers there more than me...

(it is usually mid afternoon
on those peaceful days)

while toweling off,
we contemplate what there might be to do…perhaps coffee or lunch.

but being together
on these days solves most of it.

i kiss her shoulder again for good luck,
rubbing her skin as i always do.

(i pray to have these moments again and again)

and i hardly remember the days before she arrived. it all seems like
a gray buzz of fog and lonely
displaced desire.

(close your eyes and remember
if you know what i mean)

self portrait; chicago

Cold Hands in January

these hands.

they once played in the sand,

building castles and fortresses
for toy soldiers that never really lived.

these hands
have swam from imaginary sharks
in chlorine filled pools,
alongside future politicians,
teachers,

mechanics,
and doctors. and thieves.

these hands
have gestured.
waved hello,
waved goodbye - and good riddance.

they've done pushups in gym class,
played the piano,
slept.

these hands
have sketched.
they've written essays on the civil war.

these hands
have seen good and bad days,

but

on this cold day in january,
they are dry
and aching
for her gentle,
familiar skin.

the innocence we leave behind is not a fair
exchange for these cold january days.

the tiger
the bee
the april tulip

THEY know how i feel.

If We Could Rise

do you remember

walking bare foot in the sand,
summer sun upon our necks.

do you remember

lightening bugs
in the august night.

or high dives.
or
low dives.

breakfast at 11am.

fireworks in the backyard.
lemonade over ice.

do you remember throwing it all to the wind
for an 88 cents take on a pipe dream.

the gypsy lady
walking toward us
with her long nails
assuring us that everything
would work out all right.

if we could only rise,
we would bring this bitter november moon
to its knees

and
feels the pleasures of ecstacy again.

even
if only for this moment.

we could.

we really could…

Fumbling for A View

he always remembered his mother's words...they rang in his ear at
any given moment.

it was late jaunuary
as he walked home from school.

as he walked past the old corner house,
he remembered his mother's words:
"don't forget to zip your coat up on the way home from school!"

and as he stepped off the curb at the end of his block, he watched the
street pass below his feet.

he thought about how the days seemed to be getting longer.

he came to the sudden realization that the weather was much nicer
now...better than it was last month during christmas break.

he made his way up the front steps of the house.

as he made his way toward the kitchen,
he zipped up his coat before his mother...

"hey buddy!"
she said,
as his tiny feet dragged dirty snow across the floor.

he put his book bag down…his mother stood smiling,
and stirring something on top of the stove.

something just out of view.

(for eric. who probably doesn't even remember by now)

We Were

we were often naked
and
we were often drunk.

stumbling through life.

we kissed
and made passionate love
through the days and nights.

they said,
"look at them. those lost souls..."

and we laughed
and laughed
and could only make more love
through the days and nights
of our lives (as we knew it).

a collection of vagabond types with
questionable futures.

we swore blood brothers,
kissing the girls all the way.

professing undying love for life,
through the stormy weather
and hungover sunday mornings...

we were young.

and
we were
out of control.

Vision

desire
has the ability to see clearly
for a thousand miles or more.

and yet,

love
is so blind.

see wisely.

McCormick & Schmick's

it was friday afternoon.

i woke up and was happy that i hadn't
gone to that party at spy bar the night before.

instead,
i just stayed home,
listened to the walls,
and read a book.

once awake,
i thank my brains for being sane,
shower,
and head downtown by cab to meet jennifer.

we chat for a few minutes,
she faxes some documents for me,
and i cab back to my neighborhood.

once back,
i make my way to mccormick and schmick's
to meet michael...we are discussing a restaurant deal he is working on.

he's already starting in to the drinks
as i approach the table.

mary is with him
and she is already talking too much,
as she is prone to do.

i watch her talk for about an hour and a half,
and decide once again
(as in so many times before),
SHE TALKS TOO MUCH.

mary gets angry when michael finally tells her that he does NOT
appreciate her opinions on a friday afternoon...

she gets up, grabs her brief case and storms out.

"i thought she'd never shut up"
he says.

at that point
the inevitable happens:
two blondes approach our table.

"are you also leaving, too, this table?"
they say in some eastern european accent.

michael says,
"not now...are you crazy? we are going to have you join us...so sit."

they do.

and we proceed in to the usual get to know you BS...

it is soon discovered that one has a boyfriend, and one does not. and
of course, the one who HAS the boyfriend is taking the one without,
out tonight...getting her mind off the recent breakup, etc etc.

it's always the same

the one who recently had a breakup
is not very talkative...but what she lacks in conversational ability,
she makes up for in looks. and the one with the boyfriend is almost
as talkative as mary...so naturally, i'm worried that michael, in his
impatience, will shoo them off before i take my shot.

fortunately, he doesn't. and as i sit here typing this story now, we are
set to meet up with them at 1100pm at jilly's...

i recall that
flying is easy....landing is what is most difficult.

i've had a hard time landing lately...i've only been
flying flying flying.

in to the late nights and through my sheets.

of course...i could stay home tonight.
just maybe.

i need an extra large runway with the most beautiful girl in town
guiding me in.

that would make the landing so much sweeter
and
easy to do.

time to shower...i guess i'm off to jilly's to try my luck.

    the new blondes
    are waiting.

Same Moon, Same Fire
(an interlude in spring)

what a feeling,
these nights...

what beauty,
these days...

same moon,
same fire.

she returned to me from somewhere in the universe.

same fire,
new heat.

feeling my heart race now,
like
it always has. from the first night,
to that last day...as she vanished.

and here
she lies again
and after so, so long,

next to me in the moonlight.

only this time...

this time
was a little different than the last.

christ died.
and he rose on the 3rd day.

i know just how he felt.

thank you sweet girl...thank you
for your angel wings
that lift me in the middle of the night.

After The After

she smiles tonight

like
that first night.

same lips
same face
same skin
same dancing eyes.

my fingers are
mine mine mine
or
so i have thought.

now,
they do nothing but
belong to her skin

though my mind is hesitant.

she has the skin
that burns and soothes.

the skin that fills and leaves empty.

the skin that mocks me on monday morning.

the skin that blossoms,
like a spring flower
under my sunshine hands.

and it is in the aftermath
that the anger is often sweeter than the kiss.

pity.

i kiss her now,
because it is all that i know.

she has consumed me
against my better judgement,

but it is now
all that i know.

this surrender,
this bitter, familiar surrender. it brings me to tears.

the wild springtime tulips
know just
how i feel.

she says,
"if i hurt you, i'm the only one who can take the pain away...and for
that i am sorry."

and i am afraid.

    like a firefly.

            at summer's
                            end.

yucatan; mexico

Remember

one of the beautiful things about life
is that no matter how long we've lived as conscious beings
it's always long enough to get the little moving parts right.
now and then we're called on to see someone else's point of view…
much like we'd like others to see ours.

and for better
or for worse,
it's always there. choices. options. decisions. and the situations
to make it work.

far too often
we live out of focus…failing to see the logic
of the passing waves. the brushing winds.

or the balance between death and dying…or living
and life.

i heard him say,
"the last thing to age is our heart."

and the first choice we always have
is to live in the moment.

that moment that makes every other moment count.

When I Lay Me Down to Sleep

you said,
"i'm so tired."

and i said,
"i'm so tired."

we are all slaves in one way or another,
and
you made me yours.

can you do this for me one more time?

for good luck.
or
for goodness sake.
or
just for the hell of it.

let us make our way to the bed one last time...

my fingers have fallen from grace
and
your eyes are the end of me.

those crazy blue eyes...

if i could touch my fingers to your face
and
show you
everything i see in my darkest nights without you,
you would scream for the face of God, himself.

the same ways i do

                    every time i lay me down to sleep.

Kelly

kelly is the new one around town. the long legged girl
with raven hair.

long,
open back dress.

she struts in,

eyes cool
like a menacing mako.

her moves,
so slow. precise.

she leans over the counter,
looking to her right...giving a motion
to the bartender.

she wants a drink

i watch. she lights
her cigarette,
the bartender pouring whiskey over ice.

i think i remember her telling me
that she was 24 years old one time...

she looks good in that dress,
with her raven hair
and long, delicious legs.

damn near brings me to tears.

yes. it damn near brings me to tears...

some girls are just like that.

and fucking them is always the thing that matters most.

it is always,
simply amazing.

                (watch out, kelly. here i come.)

Night Made of Stone

it is a night made of stone...cold and unforgiving.
hard,
yet cracked.

the roads have grown tired,
and the skies have revealed something red
and terrifying.

flowers can no longer be seen to leap
from the ground.

my eyes are blind
from looking in to the sun.

my lips search.

kiss me
kiss me
kiss me

remind me
that you are passing through

                       just like i am passing through

and lookingfor sex to save me as i always,
always search for something more...

from my window, oak street; chicago

Deep in A Dream of You

i wonder where she is now

as the snow falls over and past my window.

i wonder where any of them may be on this night...all of the ones that
have come through this door.

the gypsy lady over on ohio st. could offer no advice
this time.

and tonight
all the writers seemed
meaningless too.

i turned on the music
and let it drift in to me.

i walked to the window once more...

the snow flakes
just seemed to fall
right in to place...like some cosmic
white puzzle in a sea of stars and concrete.

aaahhhhh...the city and my red room.

if only it could really be THAT way.

but it is more
like the aftermath...

the snow drifts.
and frozen,
muddy roads
come after the initial beauty
of that first snowfall.

i'm deep in a dream of you
but
there is only that feeling.

the feeling of hope
                    of
                            that initial beauty.

those desperate moments
before we become muddy,

and drift and
freeze

like the snowfalls of this never ending, gray

chicago winter.

the end of my street; chicago

April 27th

and
spring time returns to chicago!

ahhhh...

walked down to the beach this afternoon. took a run north to north
avenue beach
then
back to oak street...walked the rest of the way

south
to navy pier
and returned home.

chicago is glorious when the sun rises again
in april...

the running dogs, slinking cats, and
beach combers stretch and yawn.

awakening from the months of gray skies
and muddy snows.

the taxi drivers leap
from their beds and take their fares
to every end of the city.

and last night
i returned home around 430am to find jacque
lying on the bed (ha ha...she STILL has that key).

spring time returns,
and some things never change...

i stretch out now laying myself to the sheets,
thinking about what tonight might bring.

and just how pleasant the summer is going to be.

Local News Cast

it made me laugh,
watching the news lady
interview a shaken resident
of a suburb outside the city.

apparently,
one of the students
at the local high school
had been brought in for questioning.

the student had been discovered
to be plotting the murder of
one of the faculty members.

"you know"
said the local resident,
"he was one of those outsider types...the type
who always wore BLACK...you know,
one of those kids who wears BLACK all the time
and just keeps to himself."

and the news lady
and the resident
spoke of the kid
as if he were already dead.

"oh,
i thought he'd get in trouble sometime..."
the suburban mom said.

"...and local residents are shocked and the students are stunned... classes will be cancelled until further notice...and the young man is in the custody of the local authorities..."

on the news the next day, they showed a picture
of the street, the street sign,
and the house where the kid had grown up.

"and THIS, the house where young steven rhodes grew up...hardly a hint of the horrors that would come to this quiet suburban community..."

then they followed up by showing groups of disinterested teens gathering
outside the school. no doubt happy that
classes were cancelled for the rest of the day.

The Meeting

"...so will you call me at 5:00 or 5:30?"

"mmmmmm"
i said, contemplating the question.

"well"
she said,
"just as long as it is before six...but 5:45 is good...or 5:30...so what
time do you think you'll call?"

(i thought about cancelling the dinner right then and there. she was
seeming very difficult to me. could she be jewish? ha ha...i never
did catch her last name)

"well"
i said,
"i'll call you between 5:30 and 6:00...how's that?"

"OK,"
she said,
"sounds good...where are we going?"

"i'll let you know when i call"

so i put the phone down
and began typing at the keys.

as i typed,
i decided that i did not much like her style.

here i am,
i thought to myself,
watching the clock...this one is not for me.

type
type
type
and the clock keeps staring down on me.
i pour myself a glass of wine,

and the clock: staring
staring
staring...tick tock tick tock tick tock...

type type type

tick tock tick tock tick tock...

and the doomsday clock
stares down on me as this new feline prepares her hair
and applies the lipstick.

ok...which black suit
am i going to wear tonight? do you think she's jewish? my mind
continued to wonder...

after i while,
i remember that clock...

6:01pm.

i'm late!

the phone rings
and it is her at the other end of the line...

"so where are we going tonight?"

the keyboard and keys chuckle at me and say,
"we'll be here when you get back."

she turned out to be jewish after all. and lived up to every horrifying
sterotype that ever existed...ha ha.

well, she was sweet in her own way though...and some man will
surely love her every ways.

when the time comes
i'll wish them both luck.

It Bears Repeating

i've said it before
and i'll say it again:

ils regardante ce que je regarde.
mais ils ne voient pas ce que je vois.

that's what these girls never seem to understand.

unfortunately,

        this will never change.

chicago

Frozen Lips

my lips are frozen
and my hands...i can't feel my own hands tonight.

i lay myself to the bed and pull the covers close
to my chin. the cats shake the bed as they jump to me
from the floor.

the clock stares at me from its' place on the shelf.

nighttime comes to me again. i lay here, restless.

all the cab rides and summer time girls don't mean a thing at this
moment.

of course, i've never found anything clever in being with the same
woman night after night.

but on a night like this, i could love any of them again.

my lips are frozen
and the bed can do nothing to comfort me.

sleep
sleep
sleep,

my only friend tonight...

please.

please come to me.

7:23am

another sunday.

only
this time,
no hangover.

no drinks last night,
                    and no women...

i walk over to the couch because
my body cannot find sleep.

i turn on the television..flip...flip...flip
through
the channels for the next 7 hours.

reruns
reruns
reruns

endless televised religion,
infomercials, and
cartoons.

so...this is what i've been missing - ??? i'd have done better trying my
luck at the bar last night. at least i'd be asleep right now. or fucking
if i'd gotten lucky.

and they say that sleeping away
hangovers on a sunday
is a waste of time.

i flip the channel and it's just more of the same...

Again

11:58pm
and i find myself on the blue line once again...back in to the city from somewhere
forgettable. the train and the tracks rumble in my ears.

and at night,
the rats rule.

they scurry through the dark alleys
while suburban youths plan the next
boring revolution.

designers are dreaming the next great fad
while yesterday's is drunk and forgotten.

love is somewhere
hovering over the city,

but lust consistently gets in its way.

this goes
on
and on
and on
and on...

signature room at the john hancock building; chicago

When The Dross is Removed

live well.
or at least do the little things that make it feel
like you do.
after all,
beauty is in the eye of the beholder.

"one man's trash
is another man's treasure."

"hell hath no fury
like a woman
scorned."

and style is still the answer
to everything.

when they take me in to the clouds,
i'll smile about the things i've left behind...but i'm also
quite certain i'll be gazing downward,

never wanting to live down there again.

i'll be wandering then...looking for the things
i'd dreamed of
while living
and loving
on that spinning rock
below.
i wonder where you'll be. or if
you'll be looking for me there too.

because two under the blanket
are always warmer than one.

and after all,
time will tell...time is always the teller.

because time is the fire
in which we all do burn.

live in color...but choose
your black and white moments.

and remember,
it's the small things that matter most.

they make the difference
every time.

I Am

sweet girl: i am both angel and animal.

with equal devotion
to both extremes.

I AM.

i am both devil and human. an angel with a tail...

with equal devotion to the things that pull me upwards
and down
in the middle of the night.

Letter to Michelle (An Update)

well...

i had a good friend in town for the weekend...one of my old roommates from the distant past. i lost my voice in the process. ha ha. plenty of smoking and drinking.

we spent 3 days laughing and talking...observing the people around us at the various restaurants we went to through the weekend. by the time i took him back to the airport, we were exhausted...but it felt good...sharing all those same old jokes and truths to life.

at one point, we were sitting somewhere in bucktown, sipping lemonade wth 2 russian girls around 530am...leftovers from the night.

by 630am sunday morning, we were over at mitchell's diner at clark street and north avenue.

the waitress smiled knowingly in our direction..."you boys are up early this morning, eh?" i laughed and told her we were on our way to church.
she laughed,
and
with what energy we had left,
we smiled and chuckled a bit.

i looked out the window of the diner and noticed some lincoln park hopeful coasting past on his pathetic rollerblades...looking very intentful on a sunday morning...

at various points throughout the weekend, we were rubbing elbows with club owners, drug dealers and social workers...oh - and one massage therapist from norway.

they were interesting nights...like all nights can be when you allow potential to seep in.

so anyways - michelle...i hope this message finds you well. i hope the juice is going down easily. i hope you are finding that moments of pleasure are coming to you more often than pain. take care.

ME ~

self portrait, Chicago

Perception

and what is
perception,
but
reality
to the perceiver.

in the attempts to understand,
we overlook
the obvious,

or
avert our eyes to
that which should be seen.

half empty
or
half full
is the wrong question...

is that fucking glass large enough???

or is this too much to think
about at 523pm,

before the night has really even begun.

She Says that The Night has Lttle to Do With Clarity. and I Say...

i've now and then
sought out truth....for what it's worth,
i suppose.

but my eyes go blind when i stare
in to the sun.

i can either go mad
or sip this drink
as the moon rises over the lake.

or perhaps try to forget about it for another day...

the night arrives
holding the hands of
jubilant revelers
in the midst of a summer evening.

once around me i realize
i am a reluctant,

                    but mildly buzzed part of the dance.

11am

and as i sit here
i notice the clock click one tick forward...

1101am

and not much to do on a wednesday - so i pull out my phone bill,
see it is not due for another week,
write the check,
stamp it

and place it near the door so
i don't forget it when i go to the coffee shop.

1104am now
and i'm waiting for anything
or nothing
to happen.

and somehow it doesn't

or won't

or can't

and boredom is oozing through the cracks
and crevices of the doors...in to the walls
and resting in the empty, dark spaces of my mind.

1106am. check my wallet...cash.

i head out the door for a bite to eat.

it's nearly lunch time.

i'm not quite hungry yet,
but it will give me something to do.

oh - and don't forget the phone bill...

There is A Little Known Fact these Days...But it is Known, Just The Same

if there is one thing i am aware of as of late,
it's that
no one really has that beautiful partner they seem to show.

in the coffee shops
in the market
in the black sports car

there is no magic
or
hidden magic
or wonder powder...99 cents to get to heaven.

no one person is truly exceptional
or wonderful
or dreamy.

there is only this quick wit
double talk
to conceal the inadequacy
of 6 fingered clowns
looking for a fix.

don't buy it.

don't
even believe the coupons in the mid week paper.

the world is overcrowded
with more people than $$$

or yen
or baht
or lire
or pounds
or whatever they're using these days
in the far corners of this blue-green globe.

what's worse,
is that these sheets of paper
representing something
or nothing…but who can know what
or how.
ants carry more originality than all the humans
combined…but that is another story
for another night.

this blue-green globe
watches as
lives and deaths
jump through hoops,
reaching for rising stars.

in a flicker,
the masses turn their eyes to
pathological heroes.

but i say: forget it.

it is but another act II
or III
or any act prepared and planned
to fool the masses.

there is no knight in shining armor
and no
ken to rescue his barbie.

and barbie. barbie?
i've met her...and she only wanted something more.

now that you have read this,
at least you
(and i)
can die knowing that
the only possible satisfaction we can know
is that we can know what we can know, and what
we know is this:

there are no mythical heroes anymore.

only the victories we can claim and stand upon
on a tuesday afternoon, and
in a moment of situational truth.

Although (a short story about orange fanta among other things)

although she has returned to me again,
this time it's more of the same.

although
at the start (this time),
she promised me more
than what she gave the first time around,
she gives almost nothing.

this time,
she says she is able to give more
(which of course, she does not).

and this time
she says she feels more secure
in herself,
and in me
(which of course she is not).

and this time
she says that her temper is under control
and she is capable of trusting
(which of course she is not).

she says
that she feels strong,
secure...more like the woman
she always believed she could be.

but

in a moment
this changes
and
she lashes out with cruel, biting words,
saying she feels that i make myself out
to be better than her,

and wonders why she should even talk to me
if i am going to make her feel this way.

?????

and most of the time,
i am helping her out in one way or another.

picking up groceries on the way over,
running out at midnight for more cigarettes,
taking the car for a wash,
commending her successes and answering her questions of advice,
(when solicited).

i've discovered though,
that when she is asking for my advice,
she is really looking for me to confirm
that her actions are "correct"...or wonderful.

and i also notice that she has now surrounded herself with new
friends who mostly tell her how *wonderful* she is (what happened to
her "old" friends whom she used to speak so highly of???).

and if my advice contradicts any of these new friends' support,
i am immediately given a cold shoulder

as kitchen drawers slam and the music i am listening to is changed
out of the player...

i end up opening a book to read
or just looking out the window over the lake.

i guess these days
these little bullets have caused me
to separate myself from the old emotions.

but what remains
is desire...the desire never dies.

if you could see her walk in to a room,
or watch her whince with pleasure
on a tuesday night,
you would understand
why i cannot cause myself to separate
myself from her bitter grip.

i walk over to the refrigerator
and she mentions that if i am going to drink the orange fanta that i
need to replace the cap tightly,
because the last time i drank it,
the next morning it was flat.

i see that there is no orange fanta in the fridge
(she never shops)
and mention that when i drank the orange fanta the other day,
it was ALREADY flat.

"it was not! why do you ALWAYS have to
argue with me???"

i fill a glass with water,
open my book
and wait for this tuesday night
to take us
back to the bed.

i'll be happy to see her whince
in the moonlight,

and even happier to sleep together
in the quiet of the after hours

where there are no new friends,
no false promises.

and no
orange
fanta.

The Rooster Stirred

it wasn't until the rooster stirred
and cackled
that i noticed the rising sun.

the rings were around the rosey.
the pockets were full of posey.

the tail was pinned to the donkey
and the cow had jumped over the moon.

the cat was asleep in the hat

and curious george was tired...too, too tired.

the dancing girls were spread around the room,
asleep and peaceful.

and
good time charlie...well - he wasn't looking
so good.

i walked through
and out the door
and took notice

only to the silence
that was that moment,

and decided it was time for a change.

In The Last Days (real or imagined)

in the last days
she demanded that i spend a lot of time
over at her place.

in the last days
she made a lot of demands
which at the time
(and still)
seemed quite unreasonable.

"can you go for more cigarettes?"
and the time on the clock was usually 12 midnight.

"can you run to the store for orange fanta
and milk?"
and she was usually talking on the phone
or reading a magazine.

"can you make some pasta and garlic bread? you know how i can
never make it right..."
and this usually required a trip to the store for more sauce (she never
shopped).

and speaking of that telephone,
she wore out the keys and handles
with all the time she spent talking to girlfriends,
real or imagined (they are all so catty).

those phone conversations of hers consisted of
venomous words,

thrown in the directions of (real or imagined) enemies...in the work place and in the streets.

yes, she and her girlfriends were quite sure that the world was out to get them,
yet they
themselves were part of a secret female society
who had the edge on all matters (real or imagined).

every poison
on earth
was justification for their
disjointed beliefs...and their hatred was equally spread to every race, creed, and religion...no one could escape their boiling anger.

(and what is she so pissed about these days?)

on that second to last night,
she started in to a phone conversation that i lost track of in its second hour. i just crept through the pages of the book i was reading.

i was startled at one point
when she proclaimed...
"what an ass-hole!"
and began to make some angry sound that sounded like "giiihhyyaaaad!"
followed up by a quieter version
and again the statement,
"what an ass-hole"
(and who the hell were they speaking about?).

if a psycho therapist
or social worker

or alien observer
had stumbled upon that room,
they'd think 3 times before getting in to bed with someone like her.

but me,
being the designated
orange fanta soda shopper
and cooker of pasta,
i could only be greatful
that i didn't have to pay that phone bill of hers. must be in the
thousands by now…

i'm only the guy who reads quietly and offers orgasms for peace and
silence night after night. but as i mentioned, that's over NOW.

as i sit here typing this,
i can only imagine how much hatred for me
is seething through the telephone wires tonight
and
from here to eternity. my ears are buzzing, so i can only guess what
horrifying stories are being told about me at THIS moment.

but i'm far away from all that now.

i wish her luck.

even though
i know it hardly makes a difference.

on to the next night. the next book. the next girl. and the next great
moment that will have me drifting

toward the never ending

                       next.

Ever Have One of Those Days?

ever have one of those days?

where stubbing your toe
upon rising from the bed was only the start.

next,
you dropped the soap in the shower
and hit your head on the handle
while bending for it.

the morning coffee felt good going down,
until the newspaper in your hand knocked it
from its glorious place at the breakfast table.

this is the time
where going back to bed and making phoned
excuses to any responsibilities for the day is necessary. vital.

i had one of those days recently...decided to just walk down to the
beach
and lie in the sun.

a plane flew overhead
and the sound seemed particularly sharp
that moment.

i looked up
because it was the only thing that seemed
to make sense at the time.

(had to watch for falling airliners...)

it was one of those days

                    and i wasn't taking any chances.

In General II

i once said,
"they watch what i watch,
but they do not see what i see."

and
today i realized something a bit more...

because i am often described as narcissistic

and to this
i believe
that the word "narcissistic"
is a term
most insecure people use to describe
people who are confident and self aware.

i have no need for egos, egotistical behavior
or narcissism.

when i walk
i know where i am going.
and when i don't,
it usually doesn't matter anyways.

self awareness
and comfort within one's skin
makes narcissism obsolete.

i look in the mirror and am happy to be me.

i get lost now and then and am glad
that i have the time for it.

living like you have forever has it perks.

Sunshine of Youth

when
we first had our tastes of alcohol,
we were 14 going on 15. not very dramatic,

unless you count the time
jeff beutel
stole his dad's miller light
and was grounded long enough
for us to eventually forget about him.

adults seemed like aliens to us. people
to fear
when we weren't laughing at them...because being young
solved every problem those adults
were warning us about.

and sunshine
was just as valuable to us as night.

this girl named ellen
ruled our world. she was 15 going on 25,
with breasts to prove it. she ran circles around
us
as we did everything we could to slide her in to one
of our hormone crazed beds.

here was a girl: old enough
to dance the night away,

and young enough to say fuck it...even
when it mattered.

but especially when it didn't.

years have pressed on since then. just as
they should. and with time
has come knowledge...with all the sweet sorrow
to go with it - ha ha.

ellen is just a memory these days. although
she eventually broke one of my friends hearts
back in the day.

i ran in to him a few weeks back. he was drinking 3 times
as much as those teen-angst days,

and every bit as nuts.

i asked him if he ever thought about ellen...

"a lot"
he said.

and we sipped our drinks well
in to the night
as we remembered
those nights
when adulthood was
only for adults.

and being young
seemed like the only thing you'd ever want
to be.

In Your Eyes (if only for this one night)

in your eyes
i see my infinite
and
beautiful dream.

standing on the shoreline
i close my eyes as we draw each other close.

upon closing my eyes,
it all begins...this beautiful dream begins.

see you in the morning.

Happiness

happiness is only elusive when we overlook the obvious,
or make bad choices.

glory and contentness are just a decision away.

a good life is the result of adding good decisions each moment the
opportunities arise..each opportunity exists between every breath
we take.

just an observation. nothing clever.

just an observation while rain drops trickle down the screen
over oak street.

and in the distance
the high rises represent
every last bit of it.

i make my way to the fridge
and pour a glass of milk.

it is wednesday

and my neighbor reminds me that the rent is due...

Having

i can walk to the water's edge
and
even jump in now and then…dance under a moonlit sky

or start a fire so large, it ignites the city.

i can reach for a falling star
and
toss flowers to the wind,

under a summer sun...

i can laugh so hard
that it shakes the leaves
in the trees.

i can run with grass beneath my feet
or
sip lemonade on a sunday morning
while breathing clean, blue air.

but from now to forever,

wanting
will always be more satisfying than having.

and don't we know it as we catch each other's glance
from across this room.

From The Confines of These Red Walls

some nights are more satisfying than others. but i love them all just the same...

state street at the river; chicago

It Rained Today

yesterday it was sunny
and today it rained

and who knows what tomorrow will bring
to this room,
to this city,
to these trembling fingers...

and as we lay in the aftermath
of a moment of passion
i whisper
so
you will hear exactly what i have to say:

"i am glad to know
this face that is yours"

so kiss me once more. lightly now...gentle as a breeze.

with memories of these lonely streets,
i do not want to be awake,

but rather asleep
with your scent
swimming through my mind.

Back to You

why
why
why

and i ask again...

why?

why
are these easy roads
so easy?

i work so hard to walk away,
but find so many
easy roads back to you.

once there,
that sweet pain
washes over me.

that sweet pain is my lord and master.

you were gone for months
and now you lie here,
asleep. yet...i'm awake...alone.

knowing that in a short matter of time
you'll have pushed me out again.

these easy roads
are littered
with the dead roses of my memories past.

your sad name rides the wind,

and these bitter roads…these bitter roads
are all
too easy to stumble upon…whether I am back to you

or not.

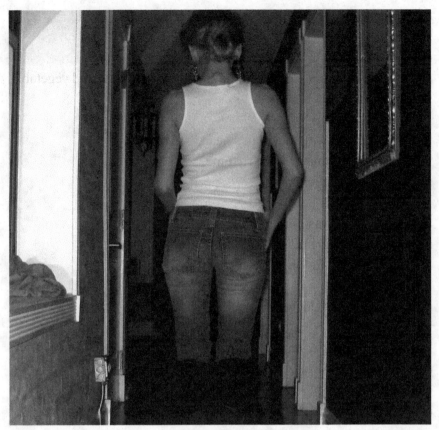

at home; chicago

Straight to My Heart

i imagined she'd be a pretty great cook.

we'd only known each other
for a few days before she began feeding me night after night.

she used to cook all sorts of magical polish concoctions...and i actually
liked most of them (aside from the cow stomach soup she once made.
or was
it cow brains? i can't remember).

there were these fried and seasoned burgers,
shnitzel,
chicken soups,
and some kilbasa dish that looked something like a meat and vegetable
salad.

they say that the way to a man's heart
is through his stomach. and trust me,
she was a firm believer.

as long as there was money for cigarettes
and after dinner drinks,
i felt that it could go on that way forever.

but one trip to the doctor changed all that.

"your triglyceride counts are way up,
and blood sugar levels,
cholesterol counts,
and blood pressure are unusually high"

he recommended a change of pace.

no fried foods.
no cigarettes.
and a hell of a lot less alcohol than we were used to consuming night
after night.
she had made her way straight in to my heart OK,
but at the expense of my blood pressure - ha ha...

so these days
there are less fried foods,

less alcohol,
and no cigarettes.

either way, the way to a man's heart has many paths.

but truly,
the real way to a man's heart is with a great ass.

and the good doctor
never said anything about that.

and it's dinner time...

Wiltshire, England

Isn't it Grand

i'm hardly old enough to know much,
but i like to think i know more than most.

i know that there have been some men throughout history that
have been serious as hell. men
we couldn't even comprehend
or understand in our most enlightened moments. but
we revere them just the same.

i find them
interesting

i like to read their quotes
and see how they apply to my own thoughts
and ideas.

BUT.

take,
for example,
a pile of rocks,
or a splish splash of oil paints thrown against a canvas. there
are people who "OOOOH" and "AAAHHH"
and pretend to intelligently discuss such things over wines and
cheeses flown in from
europe,

although they probably were shipped in by an 18 wheeled truck
from upstate NY.

i mean,
i'm sure that good intentions were behind
the great wall of china. the golden gate bridge. or even the border
fence slowly building between us and mexico.

but in the end,
who really cares. i stood in front of stonehenge
and found it visually appealing,
but was hardly driven to tears the way some 19 yr old nuveau hippie
type
was,
sitting on the ground,
strumming out some beatles tune on his 3 string guitar. (by the way,
this scene actually repeated itself when i stood in front of the main
temple
at chichen itza).

in the end,
it's just me (or you)
seeking to understand ourselves

and how to best live each minute without completely melting down (this is
a real trick...and admirable for those of us who
actually make it for years on end).

i mean,
i'm glad for the things of art
and mass movement,
but there is also something a little icky about how it affects
our worlds today.

but anyways,
as mentioned,
i'm hardly old enough to know much (although
i'm getting up there in my years),
but i like to think i know more than most.

sometimes i laugh when talking to sharon,
"if you don't know what to think about something,
ask me and i'll tell you",
i'll say.

to this
she rolls her eyes
or simply ignores me
as one
or both of us prepares the dinner of the night.

perhaps one day
people will seek to comprehend me. to understand
the reasons for the words
and the pictures,

laid out for the world to see.

"at first it was about me. then it was about women. then it was about good and
fancy love. THEN,
it
was finally
about me again",
i'll shout from the heavens.

will they hear me? do we hear
the others long past?

perhaps not.

but until then,
the great temples stand. great civilization fall.

and all the while
we're just looking to get a grip on it,
as it inevitably slips away
in the strum of a nuveau hippy
still living without a clue.

we're all fucked.

ha ha ha ha ha...

That Fucking Man Place

in the never ending battle
between men and women,
there is
one thing never considered in the psyche
of the man: someone
or something is ALWAYS gunning
for him.

from the playground
to the boardroom,
and all the places in between,
we have always been harrassed - or forced
to harrass
in order to keep our hierarchy
in place.

by the time i was in 8th grade,
i had to fight my way past
dennis hanley (easy),
dickie giles (a bit harder),
and marc shauer (the toughest challenge of all).

by the time i reached high school,
my place had been established,

and no one really fucked with me
aside from the upperclassmen
i dodged until they each graduated
one by one.

but part of being in my man place
also required that i fuck with other people. a downside
of each right of passage.

in,
and through college,
and forward in to manhood...

in a man's life,
about every 3 months or so,
a new person
or challenge emerges. a threat
to fear,
or to goad in to fear.

not fucking with someone could
lower your status. and letting someone fuck with you
could do even worse.

as i get older
these situations
are replaced by new challenges. new people
or situations to fuck with,

or be fucked.

and as a man,
you have to use your lessons learned
to pick and choose the battles that can make or break you. you have to
choose the right car,
the right women,
the right career...

it's nerve
shattering at times...and other times,

it simply eats at your stomach
as you manuever to the position of smartest
strength.

what most women can never comprehend
is that this ongoing buzz of fear
consumes the male species...all while trying to keep
your job working,
your income coming in,

and
the sexy girls
properly sexed.

now...none of this has ever caused me to
beg for mercy. on the contrary,
i've embraced this ongoing battle for my place
in the universe.

sometimes
you just have to think something over until
it all makes sense.

and this makes sense to me.

men.
women.

the ongoing battles,
and the ongoing fucks.

so
girls: next time your man

comes home a bit distraught,
tell him to suck it up
and remember what he's learned.

once he's put down
the first drink of the night,
remind him what a man he is.

then let him take
all he's ever learned,

and remind you too.

because by morning
he'll be back out there in the world.

fighting
for every inch.

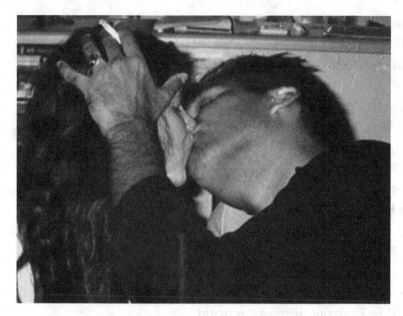

chicago (photo courtesy of melissa)

I Hold You

at 3am

i hold you tight,

as if
for dear life

and
kiss you
as if i may never see the sun again.

thank you sweet girl
for your sweet skin and surrendering soul.

it's refreshing,

and just what i needed in the middle of this old
and dusty night.

Over Iceland

Getting Closer

by the time you finish reading this sentence
a million people will have died.

by the time you think that over,
a million people
will have orgasmed,

alone
or with their lover.

things
often end
before they have the chance to begin.

a spark,

or a dulling
of the blade.

mona lisa
never smiled...she only knew.

and then
she didn't.

you receive
a note from an old friend
you never fucked. a kiss from a new stranger
you wish you could.

best to do it when you can. because
when any of you look
back,
you will have always had
THAT.

most of us
are in
and out before God has the chance to tell us,
NO.

yet
many hesitate, as that devil
tempts us
so.

look closely. the grass looks greener
after the rains.

and there's something so real
about that girl upon the stage. that man
upon the floor. those children,
running in place.

things are moving
at an ever increasing pace.

faster.
faster.
faster.

a million teenagers
singing along
to lyrics
they'll understand
only much later
in life.

game shows.
talk shows.

reruns
spinning in my brain.

"fuck you"
someone said to me the other day.

and it sounded like music
to my ears
as i lazily walked away.

see that old couple
celebrating their 50th. the family
in graceful applause.

who really knows
what happened in all those years. even the couple
seems a bit confused.

but it's happening just the same.

by the time you finish reading this sentence
another million people will have died.

by the time you think that over,
another million people
will have orgasmed,

alone
or with their lover.

another million
crying out,

or celebrating it all.

a note from old friend.
kisses from an enemy.

a new tune running to the top of the charts.

TAKE IT AWAY BOB. none of us are headed for hollywood.

sit and spin. lock it in. double
jeapordy is the answer for the day.

people never
really know. and neither
do you.

people are fucking
and dying
every second.

just please...don't fuck
with my view.

and while we're on this subject,

fuck you
too.

and yes.

THAT,

is my final answer.

until
we meet again...

reykjavic; iceland

Our 4th Dimension

sweet girl,

please don't forget that i'm the one who could never get it
quite right.

although it was never for lack of trying.

i've never been baby smooth
like the average boring white male,

but i've managed a certain flair from time to time...sometimes
even when it counted.

and even though you may not have noticed,
i don't seem to fit in with the rest of the landscape. that checkered
endlessness
which lays out before every young
and eager soul.

up and down lakeshore drive,
to and from work,

i see the faces of the hungry
and the hunted...none
so bored as me. none
so painfully aware of everything
that ever was

or was not.

i have a weakness for animals,

yet
when confronted with a fallen human,
i've often hesitated before offering a hand.

("if i were him
i wouldn't want anyone touching
and/or helping me"
i'll think to myself)

i've never been one to enjoy any of the hours between 9am
and 5pm. in fact,
my best thoughts...my best moments...my best feelings
come mostly around
or after midnight.

even better with a drink in my hand
and nothing to do the next day.

i like napping in the afternoons. i like
looking out the window. and unlike most people,

i enjoy solitude
and aloneness
when my spirits are down. i'd rather not be a bother
to people when i feel i've had quite enough.

i like sitting in crowded restaurants
alone with a newspaper,

as the rest of the mad world rushes on.

i dislike hollywood movies...the faux starlets
with their faux talents. i dislike tv,
pop music...and i almost NEVER find the featured
gossip rag girls attractive (jennifer connelly,
leatitia casta,
and estella warren being the exceptions - but then again
they don't feature those girls)

i like the underdogs. the forgotten. the subtle damned.

when a certain sport team is SUPPOSED to win,
i always root for the other guys. ALWAYS.

i read the newspaper
front to back every day but sunday. and i'm usually
engrossed in some
or other book at most any given time.

at work,
when someone excitedly says,
"hey - did you see that (insert absurd, ridiculous actor/actress)
movie???"

i usually pretend i didn't hear them and
continue my work. or i shrug it off
and mention
i may see it some time,

knowing full well
i'll never even consider it.

sometimes
i think something is wrong with me,

yet when i think hard about it,
i'm certain and convinced that there's not.

then again,
i'll never add up to the majority of my peers.

so sweet girl,
when you look on that horizon line,
please know i'll never fix myself
out there.

if you can tolerate
my mild intolerance,
we'll continue to get along just fine.

because i'm always trying
in my own simple way.

i can act like a human
when it really counts...

and when we're alone,
which i'm hoping is often,

i'll be that frisky,
sex charged animal
we all wish to be,

as the sun sets
or the moon rises

and the universe of our 4th dimension
gathers in.

G-Force, Steiner, Leslie/Lana/Lolita

greg.

we used to call him "steiner".

he was half jewish
and half italian. an odd mix,
to say the least.

but he used to go and on
about how he had the best of both worlds. italian amore
and jewish drive.

he stood about 5'6". but when he looked in the mirror
he saw nothing but
6'2"...half man,
half stallion.

he'd often
bombastically
bloviate
about his sexual prowess. his length,
his stamina,
his magical
magnetism.

the way he talked
you'd think he could impregnate a woman
simply
by staring in to her eyes.

one summer,
through strange circumstance,
he ended up moving in with us.

"3 months"
he said,
"and you guys will learn the ways of the G-force."

"it's only for the summer"
i thought to myself...

he came in,

with his boxes
and bags...strobe lights,
black lights,
empty wine bottles (as decor),
posters of women in bikinis
laying next to black panthers
and such.

i can't remember
his girlfriend's name
that summer,
but it might have been leslie
or lana
or lolita. something
with an L.

she was quite a bitch - i do remember THAT.

on most nights
i could hear him through the thin walls,
pleading with her over the phone,
"c'mon over. i'll make you some food. i'll

take you to dinner. i promise i won't (do this
or that)...blah blah blah."

if she came over
it was even more of a spectacle. she never said hello to
any of us. she'd walk right in,
past us,
through the kitchen area and
in to his room.

the door would slam shut.

soon,
he'd be playing phil collins,
bob seger,
or some other cheesy music melodies
as the arguments began.

"do it this way...no that way...no,
that's too hard...you call THAT fucking??? you
little puss...do it RIGHT!!!"
we'd hear her screaming.

"sshhhh...shut the fuck up,
my roommates will hear you!"
he'd whisper
(a bit too loud).

"fuck you. do it right
or i'm going home"
she'd often say.

sometimes she'd stay all night...on others,
she'd storm out

past us
as he zipped up and buttoned, chasing after her...

we'd laugh
at her on the way out,
"what's up with the G-force? too much
drag tonight???"

he'd return to his room,
the music low,

and occassionally we'd hear him dialing the phone. no doubt
calling her to mercifully return.

G-force,
it seemed,
was not much of a force at all.

when we were out at night,
he'd still go on and on though.

"where G-man is,
so is the party!"

and if a girl happened by
he'd say something like,
"hey sweets...how about some sweets
for the sweet!"

he'd laugh
as if he had the world by the balls,

but we mostly rolled our eyes,
counting down the days to the end of summer.

he'd go off on how he knew
the best clubs,
the best restaurants...and would some day
drive the finest cars (at that time,
he owned some unrecognizable pile of garbage
with a license plate that read "GIVE ME1").

one time
he "stole" his father's car
and proceeded to crash it. no one was hurt...but i'll bet he took a
beating
for that one. emotionally,
if not physically.

we told him it wasn't such a great idea,

but he went on about how leslie/lana/lolita
would have nothing less than he driving her around in his father's car.

"the crazier
they are,
the better they fuck."
he once said.

i had to agree on that.

but i still did not care for him.

after that summer
we split ways with little-g (force).

the rest of us hung together...even to this day.

as for greg,
last i heard

he'd bought a harley davidson
three times his size. but that was some years
ago. most likely a purchase
prompted
by a woman searching
for italian amore
mixed with jewish drive.

something like that.

i sometimes wonder about him...and people
like that.

people often
call me strange...but compared
to some of the other people out there,

i don't even come close.

The Comforter Told Me Everything

she slipped out
a little while after we'd made love. hard love...then easy....

i was in the kitchen doing something
as she whisked past.

"i made the bed up...will you call me later?"
she said,
planting a kiss on me.

"sure thing"
i said.

in the bedroom,
i noticed what so many of them seem to get wrong.

you see,
my comforter is a full,
plush comforter made by some
special designer...it was a Christmas gift
some years back
and i take special care of it,
taking it in to the cleaners regularly to
have it cleaned and shaken...fluffed up,
so to speak.

there are tassles
at the bottom,
to let you know which end of the comforter
is to go at the foot of the bed
(the tassels go at the foot).

and she,
like so many others
made the bed up with the tassels at the side...

the right-hand side,

and NOT the foot.

there was one ukranian girl,
ilona,
who,
as sweet as she was,
always made the bed up with the tassels
at the top,
which always annoyed me in the night.
because at some point,
one of those tassels would find its
way in to my ear...or worse,
in to my mouth.

and in the middle of the night,
i'd be struggling with the comforter,
turning it like a wheel,
using my toes, feet,
hands, and knees to give it a spin
in the right direction.

i'd always vow to let them know the proper
way to make up the bed,
but would refrain,

because then i felt it may be taken as if
i expected them to make it up.

all this,
after giving themselves to me...such a dilemma.

i can't even begin to tell you about the one who insisted on sleeping
with our heads at the foot of the bed...this one instigated many-a-
nights of confusion and frustration...but she had to have her way.

well - i know i've been a fool
when it comes to women,
but i don't give up on them,
or me,
on account of that...i mean,
who knows...the next one might be better.

and for that matter
writing about it seems futile.

but i do it either way...i mean
who knows...maybe the masses of the world will read this one day.

FAME.

and as far as these matters go,
even a shot in the dark
is better than no shot at all...so here i go
again.
tap tap tap

at the keyboard again
as i look around to see no blonde girls in sight.

but as i think back now,
i do remember jacque (a brunette),
and the first time

she left in the morning...she'd left
after me. i had someplace to be.

as i exited,
i said,
"there's juice in the fridge
and not much else...help yourself"

when i returned home later that day,
she was gone.

but the comforter...the comforter
was made up with the tassels
AT THE FOOT OF THE BED!

now damn,
why couldn't i keep her?

after all...she might have been the one. hmm.

maybe. just maybe...

i know her
number is around here somewhere.

In A Way, For Carolyn

it was a smokey restaurant opening over on halsted,
near armitage…a lively part of town.

i walked in with the usual crew of the time

and was surprised to see an old champ,
ted,
working the room.

he had gotten a job
as a waiter there, and we were glad for it because he was eager
to take care of us with
plenty of drinks and women.

we had plenty of dunhills
and met all the night players,
shuffling through that the room.

of course the night would not be complete
without a good woman,
and ted was so kind as to deliver
the best one that night…blonde devil with the longest legs in hell.

when she entered the room,
it is an understatement to mention
that everything stopped…she seemed
to know everyone there.

i watched carefully over my drinks
and through the smoke to see who she
may have in her sights.

the night pressed on
and it wasn't long before she was introduced
at our table.

"this is carolyn"
ted said.

"hello", i said.
reaching my hand for hers.
i handed her a dunhill
and she took it. with grace...

i lit it, and asked her how she was connected
with all these people here.

she told me she was thinking of opening
a place here in the city
and had been working her contacts.

"so who are you leaving with tonight?"
i asked, laughingly.

she was strong.

"i haven't decided"
she said,
grinning.

later ted told me she was interested in
having a drink with me after the opening.

i asked her to join us
at a nearby spot

and of course she said yes.

we stepped in to her car...she drove with
her foot to the floor,
and took turns at maximimum speed..all without
expression or fear - now that was blonde-class.

i looked her over
upon arriving at the next spot
and figured:

'if she loves like she drives
and lives like she smokes,
it is going to be an interesting night'

well, in fact,
she loved like she drove,
and lived like she smoked,

and i don't know what hit me
but
i knew i was well over my head...

she had chicago in the palm of her hand
and was well aquainted with the night. she was
a butterfly in august...last call
on a tuesday night. she was jazz,
she was rock,
she was a tulip in spring...stunning,
long,

and did i mention blonde?

she was a cook,
a lover
and a slippery thief...a true woman. in all its sense.

her specialty: angel hair pasta and pesto sauce

she
was
good.

since then,
i've been over my head a few times,
but never like that.

even something as simple as
cooking dinner together
would turn in to a night of whiskey abandon,
hanging from the ceiling
or attacking the moon with paint brushes and rainbows...

she was interesting
and
she was stunning...and sometimes, simple.

i hear she is married now
and giving her all to someone new...but perhaps
not like those nights.

i saw her recently. she smiled
and asked me how i've been doing.

"well...i've never been the same"
i said laughing.

she smiled at me,
asked for a dunhill

and with that,
said she was late for meeting

someone...strutting away
like that beautiful alley kitten.

ah yes...those were the days...before ted left for L.A.,
jim decided to take on the cuban mafia and
tom left for springfield, IL...

so through the smoke filled nights
and in to these fleeting beds,
in a way,
this is
for her...

to carolyn.

she showed me the ways of a kitten,

pouncing, loving, sleeping...licking it up before

and afterwards, too.

I'm Better Off Being The Other
Guy (so yes, bring the drama)

"i'm having trouble with him again"
she said.

"what's new"
i said,
lighting her cigarette.

"dammit",
she said..."this is so fucked up."

"we make our own cages,
even if we make them with golden bars",
i said.

i poured her a drink
and she took it,
exchanging her cigarette to her free hand.

we eventually made our way to the bed
and in the morning she slipped away early.

"i want to get home before he gets back in to
town today...he'll freak if i'm not home when he gets there."

i lazily drifted back to sleep and dreamed of
another world where people are not such a fucking mess.

yeterday,
another one told me about how jealous her new one had become over
something to do with me...

'at least he's got you'
i thought to myself...but is that such a
thing to have? are any of them happy?

i never seem to keep them,
but they never seem to fully go away either.

and being the guy on the side has always
been the easier path.

the one girl i actually committed to
in the most recent past
only turned out to be a disaster...and we talk
now and then as she is getting on with her life.

it won't be long before she has a new one too.

and
i'm sure not long after that, that he'll have a
problem with our friendship...and not long after
that, she'll be slipping away in the early morning so she can get home
before he does,
                    undiscovered...

and it's all for the better. in a relationship,
i have to wonder who is out there
tugging at their strings.

so to all you women out there having trouble
with your men,
here is a patient, but non-committal ear
and a lazy bed
just waiting to hear from you.

i'll even provide the wine and dunhills.

bring me
your drama. but bring me your legs
too…

OK

so i did it.

i know.

i got back together with her again
as if
i'd
perhaps forgotten something the first time around.

???

you know how it is...so tempting
to reach for those dancing eyes
and smashing hands.

oh,
but she was good last night...don't get me wrong – ha ha...

damn,
she has the face of a devil...that should've told
me everything the FIRST time we'd gotten together.

but a devil face has a way of
revealing the demons inside,

and reruns
always seem funnier the first time around.

it is for this reason that i sit here
tapping the keys with my triumphant vow:

no no no no no no more...if she rings me up again,
i promise to the angels of heaven i'll
never walk through her door again.

...but the phone rings. it is her...

"hello lover...i miss you...can we have a drink?"

It's You

and the one thing i know at 347am
is

it's you
it's you
it's you

and by the sweetness of your breath
and the wiggle of your toes

it's you
it's you
it's you

and your smile in the moonlight
tells me that
it's me.

kiss me
while there is still time

because,
with heaven on my side,

it's you
it's you
it's you

and with every breathless moment
between these sheets

it is only you.

5'8"

she stood there.
as dangerous as they come.

perhaps
even moreso than most.

5'8",
and nearly 6ft.
in those black heels.

she lit her cigarette
like an angel who'd somehow taken a wrong turn...

expelled from the holiest places
only to terrorize
unsuspecting men
and simple housewives.

she is 5'8"
of circumstances, situations,
and drama.

she comes wrapped in a devil shell
of blonde hair and never ending legs. red nail polish that puts that
special fire in her walk.

she comes with fingers
that would bring
the most terrifying mad man
to his knees.

she holds her cigarette
and drink in one hand,
sipping ever so beautifully
while carrying a conversation,
if nothing else,
with those striking, startling eyes.

and that is a special kind of fire. a special kind of red-class.

she looks men over
like she expects something first.
she has a girlfriend
nearly as stunning as her,
and together
they are all sorts of
long legged, expensively perfumed trouble...

scouring the cafes and restaurants
of the neighborhood,
most of the time with a man in tow,
bags of boutique shopping under their arms.

she sits at the coffee shop with me
now and then,
talking about some sucker who
will be taking her to some
magical sunset island for a weekend getaway

and
somehow or other,
after those first nights,
she has never given herself
back to me.

i saw her walking today,
alone

but over-flowing with shopping bags,
no doubt on her way to some fantastical place.

she was laughing on her telephone
as she walked past me on the sidewalk.

she is one of the most
alive women i've ever known.

i wish her luck

hell,
i wish luck to any man who
crosses her path.

LOOK! there she goes...

Communication and Advertising

i never turn on the tv
because i become aggravated
with the bombardment of information
that attacks me at every moment.

"I'M TONY PARKER,
AND MY REVOLUTIONIZED DEVICE
WILL ADD YEARS TO YOUR LIFE AND
SHED POUNDS FROM YOUR FRAME!"

flip...

"...and in other news, terror visited a quiet suburban community as..."

and there are always disinterested teens in the background of these
news stories
with annoyed housewives saying,
"this just doesn't happen in OUR community."

ha ha ha

and of course,
the alternative is just walking out the door
to see crazy mary down on state street,
begging for quarters as she advertises a breast.

then, there's the watcher,
who just watches and laughs
at everything that passes his eyes.

then there are the buses,
passing with all sorts of ads about
magic potions,
financial advice,
and information about
some sale that has already passed.

i walk in to the coffee shop and
there are signs everywhere for
take home mugs,
pre-wrapped beans,
and warmed over cd's...
at every given moment i am confronted
with supposed choices that will change
my life for just a matter of 19.99 a month,
or perhaps a one time charge of 9.99

hmmmmmmmmmm...

i return home in the late afternoons to
pick up my mail.

"KNOW THE TRUTH ABOUT RISING INSURANCE COSTS!!!"

this too gets discarded as effortlessly as breath itself.

i'm only glad the call girls
in the neighborhood do not advertise,
other than to hang out at the high priced
martini bars around the corner.

but at least they don't walk the streets
hustling...

there is a guy who sits at the corner in
front of the barney's store
who comes out when the weather is warm.

"FREE ADVICE AND INFORMATION"
is what his sign says
as he sits there reading a book with his dog.

i've never asked him for advice
but
i'm sure i could tell him a thing or two.

and for that matter, he is the one cat in the neighborhood
i can respect...

i am approached by a green peace volunteer...
"do you know what is happening in the
forests of the world?"

with my newspaper in hand, i chuckle...
"go ask that guy in front of barney's", i say.

Sometimes it Solves Itself

"you fucking bastard!"

she was in one of her moods.

we had rented a house on the lake in a small michigan town.
south haven. i needed to get out of chicago for a few days.

perhaps she's hungry,
i thought...it's way after breakfast time.

"i can't believe you the other night at dinner!
you avoided talking to EVERYONE!
and anyone who was nice to you,
you pretty much IGNORED!"

hmmmmmmm...

but they were all so boring. all that suburban shopping talk....and the
gossip. my god – all the gossip,
i thought to myself, barely looking her way.

who WERE those people anyways? i barely remember...

i sipped my juice

"and another thing! why did we have to leave so fast after dinner???"

"i told you that you were free to stay,
and i meant it"
i replied

"WHAT??? WHAT???"

i'm not sure why i bother talking back when she is in mad-dog-mother-mode.

"i wanted to stay...and do you actually think i wanted to be there with you acting that way? fucking snob dickhead???"

i didn't respond,
but was thinking how i never wanted to go to that dinner in the first place.
i even told her she could go alone...

but she wouldn't have it. she insisted that she wanted to show me off to her friends...and how eager they were to meet me – blah blah blah

what's worse, is they are not even friends of hers...only people she has chosen to impress these days. some catty suburban co-workers and dopey business men with fake rolexes...or worse: movado – ha ha.

outside our rented home
the world seemed so peaceful...the wind through the trees.

"i'm hungry!"
she said.

"i figured that"
i said.

"now what the hell is THAT supposed to mean?"

it was time to feed her. quickly. her paranoia had set in.

we went for breakfast...i had 3 slices of french toast, 2 eggs and fresh squeezed orange juice.

she ordered an omelette
and iced lemon water…oh, and texas toast, no butter.

it looked good
and i wondered if i should have ordered
that instead.

"i can't eat"
she said….still fuming over the other night.

"you should. you'll feel better"
i said.

"i STILL can't believe you the other night"
she said.

"you will,
and if you don't,
you should...and when you do,
trust me,
you'll feel a lot better..."

"let's get out of here"
she said.

"i want to read the paper before we leave"
i said.

"god-dammit"
she said,
always fucking thinking of yourself, eh?"

"well ONE of us has to"
i said.

she shot a look at me that would
bring down an elephant...God, she is beautiful when she is angry...
those blue, blue eyes.

"here - it's the travel section...look we can fly to the mountains up
in arizona...doesn't it look pretty? we can visit your parents while
we're there..."

"oh yeah"
she said,
resituating herself in the chair,
brushing her hair back with her right hand.

"that is beautiful...but fuck my parents. i don't need to see them."

"let's go over to the grocery store and get some champagne...hit the
beach for the rest of the afternoon", i said.

"oohhh - sounds good",
she said.

i payed the waitress and left her
a 4 dollar tip...grabbing a book of matches
on the way out.

we hit the beach with 5 bottles of champagne,
2 packs of dunhills and a bottle of red wine
we'd save for dinner. it was 75 degrees and sunny. wonderful.

i poured her a glass,

and as the waves came in
i told her this funny joke
i'd heard the other day.

she laughed and told me one
that wasn't too funny,
but i laughed anyways...

"i like these moments with you"
i said,
"forget all those day time people...i just want our nights...and
afternoons on the beach."

"yeah",
she said,
"you're right...this is the best."

"feeling better?"
i asked.

she kissed me.

she
was feeling better
now. i like her much more this way...

i poured her another one
and we watched the sun set.

later
that night, i cooked dinner,

but burned the parmesan tomatoes
on one side...i gave her the good ones.

"i love you"
she said.

"see how simple life can be?"
i said.

a little buzzed, we manuevered the car to the video
rental place
and fell asleep half way through the first movie.

we woke up late the next day, and the rest of the weekend was
beautiful...

"no more dinner parties"
i said on the ride back to chicago.

"but i want you to be friends with my friends!"
she said.

i looked in the back seat and saw
that i'd saved the travel section
to that arizona resort.

...we MUST plan something soon. i'm always thinking of ways to
keep her pleasantly distracted.

we seem much better off when we're alone together. no outside forces,

and no suburbanites
or fake rolexes to muddy up the view.

cooking at breakfast time

A Place for Everything

the sun belongs to the sky

and diamonds to the hand
of the possessor.

fire belongs to the earth
and ants,
to the hills they conquer.

the cross belongs
to the heavens,

and the machinest working 3rd shift is so precise.

living
is a greater miracle than birth. trust me, i know.

but death...now that i am not
yet sure.

some evenings are
like a broken pen,
the point
smudged up
and useless.

every kiss
is a hope for the next...or a return
to the first.

and as always,
and always will be,
it can be easier
than we think it to be.

so roll your sleeves up,
scramble the eggs,
and stir the bacon.

pour yourself a glass of juice,

and be glad that you have another day
to decide what parts of these nights you
will use as a springboard to the next.

breakfast was always my specialty. and surviving
has always been the only option.

Heavenly Agreement

i turned out the lights at 12:45am

and was thankful
for that moon
that keeps on rising.

i wondered
where he gets his inspiration.

i suppose he's got an agreement
with the sun…

they need each other in order
to exist…dancing in each others wake
for these billions of years.

"will you be my sun?"
i asked her…

"you are such a wierdo"
she said.

i just laughed really hard
and kissed her good night.

The Rotation

the kittens we chased
in the early days
have moved on to other things

and i see them now and then.

sometimes they look burned out
and sometimes
they are married
or
divorced
or married, separated,
and looking for their next big cat.

sometimes none of this has happened
to them and they are working retail
in some specialty boutique
or worse,

in a department store.

some wish for the old days,
and some don't even speak to me.

although we have shared
the most intimate of acts...they
just look past me or around me,

perhaps embarrased that they
have begun to drip and sag.
the wrinkles showing the years

as the dreams they sprouted
never grew.

there was this one sex-kitten we used to call
"chiffon"
because everywhere we saw her
she always had some very silky,
sexy chiffon top on...but she never
spoke to any of us. we had names for her other friends too.
there was,,
"black lizzie", "the stomach", "candy-ass", "boyfriend/no boyfriend",
and "the follower."

yes,
for each of them,
whether or not they ended up in our beds,
we had a name to identify who
they were in relation to the scene.

well - the follower disappeared. candy ass too. boyfriend/no boyfriend
moved to seattle, and black lizzie became a chicago cop. not sure
what happened to the stomach...but she was the one that made it in
to my bed towards the end. can't remember her real name though...

as for chiffon, she is now working at an obscure bar,
behind the counter...she must be 32 by now.

pity.

in the past 6 months,
i've gone through 7 full grown kittens,
all in their early 20's who feel that
they have this city by the balls.

and i chuckle when i hear their
las vegas and miami plans...and how they plan to settle down by
age 28,
married with a child in the suburbs.

i tell them the story of chiffon,
and others...like melanie-mellons,
cindy the stripper,
tank girl, etc etc etc...

"but i'm different"
they always say...
"i've got a boyfriend in law school
and when he graduates we are going to get
back together and get married...by then, i'll
be 27...it's perfect"

blah blah blah...this scene grinds
and rotates felines
like a 500 dollar blender from bloomingdales.

i met william for dinner last night
and told him that the scene is changing.

after dinner we made our way to cactus
over on state near maple street.

3 kittens,
pumped out
puckered up
and dressed to kill
sat at the next table, scoping the place
for some unwitting sucker to by them drinks.

"not tonight"
i laughed to william..."let's get the hell
out of here."

we finished our drinks and
walked our separate ways.

i walked past whiskey bar on the way home
and saw "stewardess jennifer"...a flight attendant
from the early days who freaked out on me one night
about...something i can't remember...only that it was winter and i
hailed a cab home around 6am.

she was checking ID's with a muscle
guy at the door,
and she looked past me as i walked by.

a move would do me good. but chicago still has me by the balls,

even when the girlies don't.

Object

we wonder
what is ever real anymore.

and in those moments of moments,
whizzing through life
faster than the speed limit,
we barely slow down
to make out the passing beauty.

speed bumps,
crossing gates and
stop signs...

rest stops,
fast food on the run,
and bus stop lovers.

roll the window down
and let out the buzzing fly.

change the oil,
rotate the tires,
and fill the tank.

clean the window,

fill in the blank...

we have miles to go
before we sleep

and tolls to pay
on our way to destiny.

bob's big boy

alice's easy diner

TRUCKER'S REST STOP...all blinking
and flashing in the moon light
of darkened highways.

the sun peeking over the horizon
and every potential disaster...

and love,
hinting
in the wake of gospel stations
or
country music of the open road.

careful.

and haven't you ever noticed?
objects
in the mirror
are always closer than they appear.

let's go back now and then
to see what we've missed.

let's remember what we're here for
as we rest up for the next leg of that speedway in front of us...

Ready

...and i've felt it in her scowl
and have seen it in her toes.

i have kissed the burning
embers of memory
and ran my lips across her skin.

her fingers dig in to me night after night

and she says she doesn't understand any
of it.

she hates me

which in this case
is love turned inside out then
upside down...

and she sometimes asks me to leave
at the height of her emotional
twistings

in which case i gather up what few things
i leave at her place
and catch a bus back home.

luckily
i always keep a book on hand
for the ride.

after all this time, i've learned the value of being prepared...

even when she calls me back and professes her undying L O V E.

Sunny Day

i set the oven temperature
at 400 degrees
just like the box says so.

preheat,
then place the frozen pizza
on the center rack.

bake it until it's golden brown.

the secret is
to cook it till the edges, where the cheese
meets the ends,
are golden brown. not the whole pizza.

because if you cook it till the whole pizza
is golden brown,
chances are high
that you'll end up with a crust
that is too hard to bite in to.

and if you don't eat the whole thing
(refrigerating the leftovers),
you will undoubtedly end up
with a pizza that is not
reheatable.

i'm a pretty good cook.

even when it comes to popcorn,
i know the little tricks to maximize
popping potential.

the bag always says
"heat in microwave for 3 minutes."

but this is flawed
because it always leaves you with
a bag half full of un-popped kernels.

she always cooked the popcorn according
to the rules.
and with always the same results. handfuls of unpopped kernels.

she gets very aggravated
that not all the seeds pop...

finally,
i told her to set the microwave to 6 minutes.

"at that length of time, the popcorn will burn!
i'm not going to set it for that long!"

"trust me"
i said.

what no one seems to understand
is that you can set a microwave
for any length of time you please.

it is the zing of the human element
that is vital to the process.

so she did as i said
and set the microwave for 6 minutes...

pop
pop-a-pop-pop-pop
                              pop-itty
                                            pop

and i said,
"when there are MORE THAN 3 SECONDS
between pops,
turn off the microwave and open
the bag."

"but why dont i just cook it for 3 minutes
and if there are un-popped seeds
we'll just put it back in!"

she always has to argue.

a primitive human trait.
"trust me",
i said.

so
the popping continued in to the 4th minute
whereupon
it began to wane.

pop...pop......pop.........pop......pop-itty.........POP.

"turn it off!"
i exclaimed,
laughing at my handiwork.

she opened the little bag
and poured it in to the big red bowl...

a trickle of seeds tumbled out.

perhaps 10 or so,
unpopped...and not a single popped one
burnt.

"i don't believe it!"
she said

"that is why we argue so much,"
i said laughing...
"when you learn to trust what
i say, the world will be a better place
for you to live in."

ha ha ha ha ha...

she wasn't laughing.

she walked in to the next room,
sat in front of the television,

and that was one of our last fights.

and she says
i take life too seriously.

to this i say
it only seems that way...i USED to take life very seriously...sticking
to the rules and
regulations,

only to be cut short and disappointed
over the lack of results.

but through trial and error,
i discovered that
written rules are only part of the process.

i have found that if you do things the right way,
with a little pizzaz
and a dash of human zing,

the rest takes care of itself. perfectly.

this leaves
me with very little
to worry about.

but she still lives in a world
where perceptions rule.

and on this sunny day
she called
to see if we can get back together again.

"are you sure?"
i asked.

"never mind"
she said...and hung up
as quickly as she'd called.

she never thinks ahead either.

self portrait; chicago

Some Are Distant and Some Remain

there are moments
that my visions
become a mirror unto themselves.

to this i have no control
over, except to
sit back and
attempt
to count the reflections
that twist
in the distance.

in doing so,
i find myself
further and further
removed
from the time machine
that just keeps marching on

as always
i reach for a hand,
or at best,
try to get some sleep.

there are many i've loved
or disdained

but
i am thankful
for every moment.

...it's the ghosts
in the mirrors
that do more than
haunt me.

or watch me
as i try to make them
out in the sidewalks of my mind.

self portrait; south haven, MI

Strawberry Moon

i find
limited spurts of interest
in things
for short periods of time.

and like her,
there is this relentless cycle,

as
i dance with
memories and desire.

or
sit at the dinner table
to reflect
on which things may be discarded next.

under a strawberry moon
i stand at the water's edge,
listening to the waves
as
i push my reflections
deep in to the sand.

i watch as
they drift
and blow
in to places unseen.

in a moment,
i feel her memories passing me by
and
in the distance,
she must be doing the same.

we
can never be
together
and yet we never want to be
apart.

but under this rare
and beautiful strawberry moon,

we
make these same mistakes
again
and again

and again.

a great bird
or a jolly green giant
could lift me higher.

but a simple butterfly
will always know more.

self portrait at home; chicago from 57 floors up

This City

i have chased for
and found love
in the corners and
high rises of this city.

i have walked the rained on streets
and even watched them bake under the summer sun.

i have seen them crack
under the strains of winter
and spit out the suburban boys
who never seem to get it right.

chicago...

i have run home
for fear of freezing to death,
slept through fires,
and drank with the insane
and the original.

i've given countless lovers back to the city
and even let a few back in.

but on this monday morning
i watch the sun rise
with a different point of view.

i look around the room
and see the sleeping cats.

the red walls are as red as they've ever been

but something has to change.

south haven, MI

Mystery Kiss

when she kisses me
she is like that
sleeping bull in my mind.

...i never quite know what she is going to do next.

there is a feather point of danger
in every way she walks

and she knows just how to smile.

those lips of hers
can shock me with electricity
or
offer me the peace

of a light house
on a
summer night.

everything about her
dances
with a dangerous
and silly beauty.

and the only thing
more hypnotizing than her
kiss
are those
gazing,
oceanic eyes.

i am tossing like
a ship at sea,

but
i am greatful

for her skin in the middle of the night.

these things
are ours...for the moment.

(and every moment we can steal from here on out...)

Where Freedom Drifts

your hands and fingers
and eyes and toes
crawl over me like a wall of ivy...

twisting
in a
loving
yet
strangling love.

i am so tightly wrapped
in your embrace
that everything just turns to black.

with every volcanic dream
i wish for you to be burned
to the ground.

and i hope for the
listening winds
to carry you away...ashes
drifting out over an ocean of forgiveness.

only there
can we truly be free.

only there can we begin again.

london

I Do Protest

i think that most everyone can agree
that given a choice,
they'd rather not be treated poorly,
shouted down,
oppressed,
blown up,
beheaded,

or have their day altered by one idealogist
over another.

i don't think that one person's desires
are less relevant than the next,
but there is something to be said
for keeping your mouth shut
when there is an urge to do otherwise.

i don't know who is in control any more,

but i'd like to think
that to a certain extent,

it is me

and you,

and the countless neighbors
waking for another day's work.

a certain level of reason
balanced with a certain level of standards
are all we need
to get lucky again...because i don't
think we're very lucky these days.

and when i say standards
or "reason",
i don't mean the kind of "reason" that lawyers,
judges,
politicians,
extremists,
gays,
straights,

homeless,
blacks,
whites,
jews,
muslims,
or the other races and creeds of the world try jealously
to define.

i'm talking about
good old fashioned manners.

i mean,
i know that a bit of the bad stuff
is inevitable,

but given the choice,
it would be ideal if people
were strong enough to choose
good
over harm. tolerance
over evil. and acceptance
over selfishness.

i hear that certain extremists
will not stop until every sort of democracy
comes tumbling down. i hear that these extremists
will not stop until mankind
as we know it
is reduced to glowing rubble, unless each individual of what remains
makes a vow to their teachings.

but i imagine
if they have their way
they'll be left with only each other. rabid,
fowl men

and a million or so opressed women
with no allowable voice.

just the way they
like it.
i don't know what the answers are. and
i'm certainly running out of questions.

but i'm hopeful
when i see one good thing
done in the name of nothing.

because to a certain extent,
we
are
in control. one
and all.

now if someone would pass
this on with the ketchup
and the mustard
and a few beers while the music plays,
maybe we'll all get lucky again. the kind of luck
that lasts
and lasts
for a good long time...

Sleep Walking

somewhere
in the corners of my mind
are unknown worlds
that i search through
for sources of
strength.

in my dreams
i find myself
with eyes wide open,

fixed
and gazing on a red sky.

there is a sweetness
there is a sadness
there is a yearning
there is a madness

i can hear my own voice in the distance
and i fully realize
how far removed from myself i will always be.

my distant voice
falls and climbs
and falls again.

and when that distance
becomes quiet,
                    it is then that i am most afraid.

the alarm clock
wakes me from its place on the stand

and
i fumble for it
with fingers that ache for
her gentle, familiar skin.

i dream so much now
that i never know it
when i have become awake.

Didn't I

i gave you something that
i'd never given before.

there were times
i gave more than i was capable,
and it only left us
angry
lonely
desparate
and wanting.

somehow,
the wanting
became greater than the having
and
the bitterness
became sweeter than the kiss.

and no words
could replace
the pain of the
day to day bullshit.

and the nights
could no longer make up
for the rest.

so here are
on our separate ends
of this city

under a cool
and unforgiving sky.

I Have, I Will

i've been
a ship
tossed upon
an open sea,

a canoe
lost in a rocky river way.

i've been a sunrise,
                              and a sleepy sunday.

i've thrown caution to the wind
and have had it thrown back at me.

there have been moments
of passion
and there have been nights of whiskey and roses.

i've kissed fire
i've seen beauty
i've ached in the aftermath of ecstacy.

and on this morning
it has been 3 days since i've shaved
and the clock on the wall
just keeps ticking away.

there is a lesson here
there is a moral here

and believe it or not, there is something of value
to be found in days of desperation.

i will find it.

i'll recognize it when i see it.

i'll use it to keep me walking.

i will not be divided by
these empty nights.

i will find a way to the hilltop.

i will find my way
through these
winding
dirt roads

and i will love again. and again.

and again…

On an Afternoon Like This

and on an afternoon like this
i wait for the sun to inch behind the clouds
of early evening...hot day in chicago.

as the music plays,
i shower twice
in 4 hours...then decide to just turn on the
air conditioning (there is a sign
on the elevator that says: "please do not turn on your air conditioners
until after 4pm for the next 3 days as we clean the front of the
building")

i look out the window,
see that the workers have hung it up for the day
and i turn the unit on...its humming,
cooling the room in minutes.

i want to dress
i want to get out
i want to head over to
TEMPO and order an omelette
with mushrooms, onions, bacon
tomatoes and cheddar cheese,
with texas toast,
hash browns on the side...extra dark
and a large milk with ice (got that?).

i keep getting distracted though

the phone rings
the cats beckon
the mail arrives

a knock at the door

and it is a young kitten
who comes around now and then

"i have a chicken and tomato
wrap from LO-CAL ZONE...wanna have half?"

i let her in,
and we share a laugh
as i tell her about my latest weekend excursion out of town.

out there
there are freeways of the city
jammed with salespeople
and mothers...mailmen and crooks.

there is love,
or no love...riding bikes
or racing out of town
for reasons unknown.

i'm glad for the chattering girl
in front of me,
and for the sandwich
she has brought to me.

and i know that
i have survived one more day,
with a chicago evening spilling
in to the sky...good days are in front of me.

i take a sip of my drink
and turn the music up a little louder.

she once told me she liked
this next tune coming on.

i finally decide to give it to her…

When The Truth

when the truth finally arrives
it is like a floodgate of emotion

as powerful as an ocean wave
or as gentle as a whispering breeze.

it should always feel this way.

your chest
will rise
and fall
with greater ease

and you will be able to breathe again.

VII.

she said,"i don't want you writing about me."

"that's OK",
i said,

"i just want to look…"

photo courtesy of jessica

We Had This Understanding
(No Questions Asked)

we had this magical arrangement...somewhat unspoken
but it was there just the same.

so whenever she sauntered in
to my place
i was always grateful.

i'd be at home
typing away
or sitting at the coffee shop
when i'd get the call.

"what are you up to? feel like a little company?"

and i'd hustle over to potash supermarket
to pick up a few bottles
as she made her way over.

sometimes
we'd sit and drink on the rooftop deck, or
sometimes we'd sit at the beach.

we'd always end up to
dinner somewhere
and she'd tell me about
this or that
young guy
who'd asked her out.

"how is he?"
i'd ask.

"young,"
she'd always laugh, "too young"

we'd laugh about
the many who chased her...she is
more than nice to look at.

and the guys
who asked her out
were always around her age...like 21
or 22...wild,
wreckless,
indecisive,
lacking in basic knowledge...or some inadequate combination
of the above.

"i love seeing you",
she'd always say at some point in the night
"you are a calming part of my life...and we always
end up at these cool spots for dinner."

sometimes i'd buy her an
outfit to wear
at one of the shops on my street.

i always got to choose
what it would be
and i'd show her off to the boys
over at…

we sometimes made our way
over to luciano's to hear lenny sing

on that piano...or to the cafe
at oak street beach.

with her new outfit
she always felt (and looked) stunning.

and in bed later in the night
she'd always claim
undying passion for me
in the throes of the moment.

i never asked her
how many lovers she had
and she never asked me about mine.

the need for exclusive possession
is what causes beauty to break down before its' time.

those were the best of nights,
watching her sleep,

or talking to her under the chicago sky.

sometimes looking at her became too much

and i'd look over at the sleeping cats
or in to the distance of the city scape
as she chattered away (she loved to talk).

and when i looked back to her
she'd still be talking

and those beautiful blonde strands
would still be in the right place.

the honking on the streets
below
and the quiet sounds
of the room
would always keep me happy.

without a future to hope for
there's never anything to worry about.

and ending the night
in each others arms
with
no questions asked,

was always a beautiful thing.

It is Miraculous Soul Out There

there is something
smoothly miraculous
when you meet a
good woman.

the way she smiles
upon first meeting
lets you know
she is going to be different
than the others.

maybe it will be a book she's read,
a movie she's seen,
or the scent of her favorite perfume.

every so often
she will suprise you
by picking up the dinner tab,
or bring a flower by in the late afternoon
(yes, men enjoy a flower now
now and then - ha ha).

it may be in the way she hums as she does busy work

or the charm of her aloofness,
that is more innocent than calculated.

it may be the way she walks barefoot whenever possible,
or spreads lotion across her arms and legs...maybe it's
the way she drips the mustard sauce every time she eats a hot dog.

other times
she will just be silent.

and the silence
will not grip you with fear,
like it does with the others.

her calming silence
tells you that every thing will
be all right for some time.

and during those glorious days
this miracle of a girl
will hold my gaze
for seeming eternities...for miles,
and for a thousand lifetimes.

i think there is a playful
and beautiful soul out there
that enters
and exits various girls i have met
over the years,

hopping from body to body
and finding its way back to me.

every time we meet
it is like an august breeze
on a hot summer night.

every time we meet
i find myself
sleepless in ecstacy.

it happens
maybe once every few years,
pleasant and calm.

"i think we've met
in some past life"
they often smile and say.

it's been a while since i've
heard someone say that.

i look forward to meeting her again.

I Want To Be A Sand Man

the fan spins overhead

and the air conditioning unit buzzes
as the sleeping cats purr.

the city sleeps

and the taxi drivers
sit at all night diners
sipping coffee,
waiting on a fare.

i envy all of them at this moment.
because here i sit
with no purpose and
sleepless on a tuesday night...233am.

the sand man
must be the only one who
will envy me at a moment like this

as he shuffles on his
assigned
after-midnight lot in life,
he comes across me

and is probably
glad that
someone else is up too...but i'm not
working like he is.

maybe i can sign up somewhere
for his job...hell,
i already sleep all day
and stay up all night.

i'd be good at that.

and he can probably use a break
now and then.

Chicago

there is a cool
and windy breeze
that rises over the lake.

the city skyline
brightens
as night time
breathes over the city.

chicago.

with its streets,
boulevards
and cafes…

it buzzes
with the pretty girls
and night time boys
looking for a master - or savior.

there are times
when
anyone

anything

any moment

can rise,
        standing
        in the face of the buildings,

                                        street hustlers
                                            and low rollers.

making a statement of beauty
in a moment of pure white passion
that always brings down the house.

i live for those moments
as i light my cigarette
on another night.

Daley Plaza, Chicago

She is Waiting On The Next

sometimes there is a crazy one. a rabid kitten gone wild.

she stands there...pressed
against the bar,

purse wide open,
ashtray full of dead butts,

fingers that fumble and reach for more.

she is more often than not
on the declining side of her beauty
which
may have been something to see for 6 or 8 years...

she is often well in to
26 by now...27 or 28,
and the younger felines are fast
on their way
to replacing her.

recognizing her new competition,
she works hard to befriend them.

they compare notes
as to how to land a sucker...the one
with the most money.

of course the sucker with the most money
is part of the process in his own way.

he soon realizes that there is a constant
influx of new and young ones to replace
the ones who are inching their way over the hill.

so he stays true to the game.

but SHE is there...night after night

ass falling out of place,
hair in need of repair,
and eyes...showing the years of smoke filled nights.

and while
society
and the U.S. economy
take their usual dips and dives
she
is still pondering
movie star magazines,
13 hour sales
and her hero who is likely to ride
in on a white horse at any moment.

it is good to take
a few moments now and then
to observe this strange being...this
girl on a *mission-impossible.*

yes,

sometimes there is a crazy one
at the edge of the bar
at the edge of the night

at the edge of her hope
on the outskirts of the twilight zone.

and in that moment of moments
she somehow believes herself to be
more sane
than anyone in the room

or
anyone she can recollect.

                   or even anyone she may ever meet.

although we are mostly led to believe
we are to live a life of boredom
and calculated insanity
we should somehow take a moment
to honor the crazy girls of the night.
for the moment, they are too old to start over.

                              yet too young to give in.

it is in this dance
between reality
and the dream
that the all too human female
wakes up one morning,

sadly
sane. inconveniently aware. yet not quite fully awake.

when i see her
i sometimes offer a drink.

of course, she rarely accepts...she's sleepy and lost in thinking
something better
is bound to come along.

blue line subway; chicago

VIII.

yes.

we are still allowed to dream in color...

pick yourself up
before it's too late.

open your eyes.

Closer to Heaven

she keeps calling now and then.

sometimes it's in the middle of the afternoon
and sometimes it is at 2am.

the calls come with less frequency now
    but
         the calls are there just the same.

sometimes she talks to me
about a new MAN she's met
and
how he'll be taking her out of
town for the weekend.

or sometimes it's a new girlfriend...how this
new girlfriend is
just so special...they really relate
and
i should really meet her sometime.

she
suggests we go for drinks.

i always decline.

"well"
i say,
"let me know the next time you go,
i may join you."

but the new girlfriends,
like the new MEN,
are always fleeting.

they never last
and she never makes it out of town.

she doesn't hold on to much
for very long.

she mostly despises
humans,
especially men…she claims that the men she meets are not REAL
MEN at all.

but still,
her beauty is a trap.

and getting away
is always like
climbing out of a soaking net.

the last time she called
she mentioned a party she'd gone to.

i didn't ask how it was,
i just said
"oh, great…i was out of town last weekend."

there was an awkward silence.

"aren't you going to ask about my party?"

"hmmmmmmm"
i said,
"i'm pretty certain how it went for you."

"...anyways"
she says,
"i met this really great girl
who i really got along with!
she is divorced like me and..."

"look,
it's late,"
i said,
"i should be getting to bed."

"i miss you."
she said.

i can bet a million dollars to ten as to what she misses:

she misses having me
caught securely

in her soaking, fucked up net.

she has seen
me lose my mind
at 3am,
            and my vows to walk out
            at least 27 times.

when i finally did it
she just said,
"i don't believe it"

the door shut behind me the
last time
and i never went back.

when you escape from
a devil's hell
their hell becomes that much more hellish.

"fuck you."
she said
in one of our last phone conversations,
"you are such an asshole."

luckily it wasn't too late...like 1130pm or so.

i didn't lose
too much sleep that night.

and on this afternoon
it is good to be free.

and good to be a little man who is
closer to heaven
than he used to be.

Contemplating Passion and Nothing
On A Sunday Afternoon

imagine
if you will
the day
someone like hitler
or picasso
or the pope
decided what they were going to do
with their lives.

while someone like
you or i
wonder what might be good
for lunch or dinner,
there are others
out there
on the verge of
glory,
disaster,

or terror.

when they pulled saddam out of a hole, he knew it couldn't have been
any other way.

passion is what makes
or breaks us...to have it or to lack it
is what separates
the newspaper clerk
from the president.

humans
live
as millions of humans live.

break downs,
tune ups,
over cooked
yet
under fed.

make ups,
breakups,
water to wine.

and two weeks vacation to keep us all in line.

with these things in mind,
i have somehow managed to keep the refrigerator
full
and i even manage to eat out a few nights a week.

there are hopes and aspirations
that must be managed
with far greater cunning than
an after school special or some julia roberts movie.

real life lasts longer than a two and a half hour film
and popcorn prices are always rising.

as the weekend winds down
and a new week is presented to me
i wonder
on this sunday afternoon
just how things are going to go.

every effort i've made to make things
right again,
i'm hopeful,
will turn right for me...maybe
my luck can turn around.

i open the windows now
and look out over the city
as the cats tumble
and play on the bed.

the red walls
whisper something,

but i don't have the patience
to listen.

a siren sounds in the distance
and every honking horn
on the streets below tell me that
the humans are out there

just like me.

in one way or another
we're all still alive.
and saddam...saddam lost himself somewhere in that hole.

and bin laden. he smiles quietly as he realizes that his fate will
surely be

the same.

Another Sunday Night in Chicago

we walked out of the movie theatre
and decided to head over to hunt club
on state street...sunday night. 12 midnight.

although the usual sunday night
spots are hopping,
it's been a long weekend
of late nights
and hard drinks that started on thursday night.

so
we decided to go
the quiet route tonight.

i ordered a rolling rock beer
and a miller light for robert.

"no jacks and cokes tonight."
i said.

we were sipping away
when a group of
silver foxes came strolling in,
black evening gowns,
black purses,
and black shoes all around.

"is it prom night at some over 40 club
in the area?"
i chuckled.

the ladies
bopped to the music,
drinking martini concoctions
at the bar.

one silver fox
kept shooting us sexy looks
which became more and more absurd
as the night pressed on.
"the girls just keep on coming, don't they?"
i mentioned to robert.

he laughed,
"what do you mean."
he said.

"look at them...4 ladies in their
mid to late 40's
acting like they still believe they are 19."

"they probably do,"
he said,
"most girls are too crazy to know that they are."

"ha ha ha..."

the most bold of the bunch
then looked over to us
and started in to a double finger
seductive 'come hither' motion,
while the dress tried desperately
to hold the rest of her together.

"oh my god."
i laughed.

i really felt sorry for them.

2 young ones,
maybe 23 or so
made their way in by now,
taking the stools amongst the silver foxes.

"i bet those 2 new ones are european"
robert says.

"why do you say that?"

"look at their shoes...and the way they
wear their hair...straight
and finely combed."

"i bet you're right,"
i say,
"i was just trying to see what you see."

so the seductive,
finger waving silver fox
keeps dancing,
grooving,
and shooting sexy glances
in our direction.

the europeans
are laughing at them now,
behind their back.

"nobody wants those silver
foxes anymore,"
i say,

"and the europeans...not even the comraderie
of females exists enough for them to make friends."

"that is good,"
robert says,
"if all women, young and old united
it would be a dangerous world,
and we'd never get lucky."

"ha ha ha!"

"so what do you think?"
robert says,
"let's go talk to those europeans...i heard one
say that her name is daniella...the blonde one...you
take the brunette."

"we'll probably have to fight past
those silver foxes to get to them."

"ha ha ha"

"forget it,"
i said,
"i should get home...it's like 2am now...i've got stuff i want to do
tomorrow."
so we paid the waitress
and worked our way to the door.

the europeans smiled
and the silver foxes danced…

and outside there was a group of
3 young ones presenting their ID's
to the door man.

i said,
"what we miss out on tonight
will be there for us tomorrow...these
girls will never stop coming."

"and they all think they have
the corner on the market,
don't they?"
said robert.

to this i laughed

and gave him the usual
high five-hug
that comes at the end of each night.

"see you later this week"
i called to him.

and he waved,
lighting a cigarette
as he did so,
making his way west on maple street
towards his place.

another sunday night in chicago
and another night of girls
on their way to
a slow
gray
fade.

(but tonight,
the silver foxes
are staying true to the hunt)

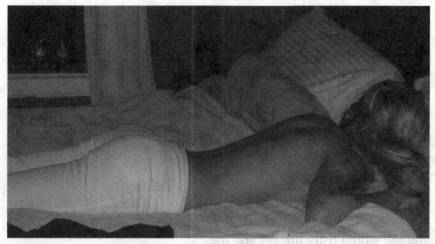

Chicago

One Shot

...and if i could just kiss those lips,

parts of me
could be saved

> or at least be given
> the sparks needed to pull
> off another day.

i see her from time to time
yet
we never speak.

but
hey,
there she goes again

hair waving

as she struts
toward me...

"most men are cowards
in the broad day light", so i once heard...

and today i am no exception.

but give me a night,
some drinks,
and half a pack of dunhills
and she would truly understand the
meaning of passion.

i'd always leave her the daytime.

i'd just want
the nights.

we would both
see how beautifully
two humans can live,
and
how the pains
can be put off for
just a little more time.

the breezes of love
carry magical dust
that make
even the most vivid rainbows fade to white.

the heat of love's glory
create the embers of memory
that keep you coming back for more.

ahhhhhhhhhhh,

if i could just kiss those lips
on a day like today.

every wild horse inside me
would rumble over a distant
and beautiful hill

closer to everything beautiful that ever was.

Fuck You!

she always
accused me of being
self involved.
self consumed.
distant.

"i like to have things the way i like them"
i said,
"is that an unreasonable proposition?"

"you always have a way of putting
things in a way as to favor YOUR point of view."

"and you would like to be the same way,
no?"

"fuck you."
she said...she was always good at saying that.

i said,
"'fuck you' is no longer a phrase you
are allowed to use when we discuss these things...
it's cop-out."

"fuck YOU!!!"
she said,
using her finger to point at me for emphasis.

"c'mon"
i said,

"have another glass of wine...let's order
some dinner."

"you are an insecure ass hole
and you cover it up by keeping people out...or
exposing just enough to...to...FUCK YOU!"

i couldn't believe it...she ran out of twisted logic.

"let's see,"
i said,
"i can sum it up...i give just enough to keep you
curious but not enough to keep you happy, right?
so why rely on me to keep you happy? find your own interests...i
showed you how to use that camera...i critique your writing....um...i
taught you the basics of cooking...just learn to appreciate what i am...i
don't cheat on you, i take you out of town when you want...we go to
dinners...i introduce you all around town...i..."

"oh you are just SOOOO great aren't you??? MISTER popularity...
mr chicago, right???"

"here is your wine,
drink it, it will calm you down."
i said,
"and here i am...right where i want to be...with you, no? when you are
just you, you are the most alive woman i've ever known. really...and
i can never leave that face of yours...i WANT to be here."

she sipped her drink
and lit a cigarette.

"what is it that is REALLY bothering you?"
i asked.

"nothing."
she said.

(NOTE: i may have insecurities
but i don't get others involved with it)

"listen,"
i said,
"i used to be pretty blatantly insecure,
but i have had years to practice another path
in life...i don't let my insecurities get the best of me anymore...i
learned my lessons far too gravely
and far too sadly...i'll never go that insecure direction again. my
insecurities really pushed people away...now other things have taken
their place...BALANCE."

i balance my attention to women
with photography, or writing...or else my extreme
sides will surely take over.

she sat
with those eyes,
sadness replacing
their usual brightness.

"you are pushing me away."
i whispered,
"you are doing it every moment you try
to control me...every time you accuse me
of everything you are trying not to be...why do you
do it?"

(NOTE: my insecurities
are like an underlying old river
with a city built on top of it.)

she cried
and,
damn it...i knew then
i could never go back.

she will never change.

i think of her often
and i think of the
ways of love
after midnight.

i can't help but remember
every
morning scent.

every
afternoon on the beach
                and
                        of course
                        every thing that can never be right.

i type here now
at this keyboard
and think of the many ways
i tried

tap
tap
tap

here is the end...time for dinner

and
i have to feed the cats.

i wish
her well,
wherever
she may be
right now.

but it would be so much
nicer
if she were here with me
right now,
quiet,
peaceful,
secure.

and no more "fuck you's."

kitty at home; chicago

The Cats

i got him in february of 1991
which puts him well in to his 12th year now

although he came from
quite humble beginnings
he has managed to aquire
a certain level of fame
amongst most people i know
or have come to meet him.

he is my cat...well my oldest of two cats
that is.

he has a way about him

the way he talks
and muses in a steady manner...

he interacts
if you interact with him
but he
will mostly snub people until

he is ready to make his move.

then
he is strangely
curious,
friendly
or rambunctious.

and when he has had enough
of human interaction
he just saunters away,
giving an acknowledging "meow" on his way out...sort
of a "thanks for the memories"
which tells you he may or may not be back.

he is the type of cat
that could possibly walk in to a bar,
order a drink
and have people offering him cigarettes
for his time...very cool.

when a girl i haven't seen in a while calls
they often ask,
"how is the old guy? does he have any
secrets of yours he can tell me?"

i got a second cat a few years ago,
much to the first one's dismay,
but he tolerates him.

the oldest one likes to take it easy
and doesn't much like the scamperings
of the younger one,
but he manages to keep the young one
in line if he gets too...crazy.

the older one will even clean the younger one
now and then,
whispering the secrets to a long life
in to his ear as he does so.

the young one likes the older one to clean him or nuzzle his neck.

but if the younger one needs anything for too long,
the older one will proceed to flip him
and send him on his way.

"ok, enough."
he must be thinking,
"i need to relax."

he keeps his gray coat well groomed,
and sits outside the door now and then.

he loves his cat naps, which he likely invented in some other life.

when he talks,
although i cannot understand him completely
it seems as if he is telling me he is sick of eating the same thing day
after day...
"doctor's orders",
i always say to him
as i pour more in to his bowl...variations in his diet
give him urinary tract infections and affect his weight.

he also says he'd like to move sometime soon,
but he enjoys being friends and likes the fact
that i keep him protected from the outside world...that
is what i've gathered so far.

my cats...i like them both differently
and for different reasons...although
they get equal time and attention.

but the older one
really has that style...he knows just how
to make his presence known.

he loves girls too...and when a new one arrives,
he sizes her up...circles around a few times
then moves in...very smooth.

he looks in to their eyes,
he talks to them,
sits in their lap

and shuffles away
when he feels the need to be alone.

i wish i were as much a man
as he is a cat...could very well be a dangerous situation...ha ha.

anyways,
here he comes now,
looking at me as he approaches.

he's not making a sound..but he looks
like he's got something on his mind.

the younger one is fast asleep
on the window sill.

he likes to look out the window
as much as me.

ahhhhhhhh...what a night.

and the cats feel it too.

well,
i've got to go now...the old guy's got something on his mind. perhaps
it's not much at all. but i do know he wants to talk...

To See

i'm often awakened in my dreams...a million thoughts
racing. an old face. a new memory. a
lost friend.

it's strange...i can fly in my dreams. but mostly
i prefer to float. hanging over the city
or countryside. contemplating
life,
death,
and love...or lack thereof.

sometimes
i dream of music. no images. just little flashes
of light
or static
which somewhat resembles an old tv on the brink. but
not
quite.

somehow i'm reminded
of the luck i've had. the friends i know,

and will always know.

i'm grateful.

in life,
we're fortunate to meet 5 people
who will come to know us
inside
and out. perhaps even fewer than that.

i've been fortunate to meet a handful of friends
who,
under certain circumstances,
know me better
than i know myself.

i'm proud to say
i've been able to repay those relationships.

i've been affected by the things i've seen. the things
i remember. and the things
i've lost.

it all counts in adding up.

and my dreams
often wake me in the middle of the night. sometimes
in angst. sometimes
in euphoric peace.

often,
i'll get up for a glass of juice. a walk down the hallway
to check on the cats.

i'll look out the window,

and wonder if anyone
will ever
truly understand.

they watch what i watch.

but they do not see
what i see.

sometimes i close my eyes...and i see
even more.

i see
so much
more.

Endless Lover

it was the time before here...before moving to oak street.

before bucktown,
but after lakeview

it was before loree,
before jewish julie,
before jessica from brazil,

and before my trip to asia

lincoln park...

living in lincoln park
has done a lot of irreperable harm
to my body
and especially my mind...but in some cases,
for the better.

i was often with the
toughest players in town
along
with
the wildest of women.

i was younger then...maybe 23 or 24.

the girls
ranged from
18 to 35...i was at that magical age
where i could still get the young ones

and the older ones
were all so intrigued…

sometimes i paid for the drinks,
and sometimes they paid.

and sundays were always about scamming
food and drinks to make it through the week
to come.
there was the time,
passed out on the front steps
of my building,
slice of pizza in my hand
at 530am...a slice from amar's - an all night
pizza spot in the neighborhood.

my neighbor woke me,
"what the hell are you doing out here?"

i sat up, looked around…

"going to work?"
i asked him.

"yeah...and you - look at you...just getting in...and no lady tonight?"

the women made it by
on most nights
but that night
i was not so lucky...that's where
amar's always came in to play...old amar
was glad when i didn't get a girl
because he could then count on me stumbling
in for a slice of his pizza.

"$3.25."
he'd say, handing me the slice and pop.

in those days
everything melted together like cheese.

and
when they weren't melting,
things were often collapsing.

always on the run.

oh yeah,
girls were-a-plenty,
but not much else seemed to make sense...not
much to hold on to.

and because
all of life is
predicated on hope
and the hope for hope,
i always imagined the next one to come along
would be better than the last...and when the new
one didn't pan out as i thought,
i was sure that the one before her
might have truly been the one.

and through it all
were smoke filled nights,
days on the beach,
afternoons at the coffee shops
and sundays of despair (as mentioned above).

in those nights
the legs seemed longer,

the drinks more grand,
and the conversations more lively.

but the mornings always revealed the truth.

i think
i had myself pretty well
fooled though.

i even believed that i fell in love
now and then...i mean,
you can't keep yourself down
all the time, right?

i ran from one to the next,

breathless.

we drank alcohol,
we ate food,
we devoured each other,
and took wild trips out of town...

new york
new orleans
texas
california
miami
key west

sometimes by plane,
sometimes by car.

east to west
north to south...just the way
some of us love...it is a way of living.

when one of them (carolyn)
proposed marriage,
i nearly choked.

"um,
ok"
i said...

we proceeded to pick out a new place
to live,
a car,
a future...what it might be like.

"suppose we really go through with this,"
i asked her one night over dinner,
"then what?"

"well then,"
she said,
"don't you think i'm beautiful?"

"sure."
i said.

"i'm yours for life!"
she responded,
"isn't that enough?"

the next morning
i kissed her on my way out
and decided to see less of her.

she found someone to marry her
within a few months...argentinian guy.

they went on to marry,
have 2 children,
and i hear she now supports all of them…

amar's pizza place closed down
and i moved to the gold coast,
then to Bucktown
then back to the gold coast
where i now reside...all in a matter of
12 years time or so.

i have to be near the beach.

my neighbors are still curious...i always seem
to bring it out in them.
and one in particular...

"where do you meet all these women?"
he once asked.

"i honestly don't know"
i said.

"always such a ruckus of sound
when i walk past your door...ha ha ha..."
he said.

to this i said,
"i guess it is about being around...i hang out
at the coffee shops,
local spots,

friends have friends...there are out of town friends,
new friends in town friends,
strangers...they're always looking for a fix
and i'm always hanging around or
available to provide it...plus
when some of the old standbys call,
i'm always around...they say 'hey, i'm in your neighborhood...can we
have a drink?'...and i'm always there for them."

the other day
my neighbor stopped by to ask a question.

the phone was ringing
as i opened the door to his knocking.

"i'll stop over to your place in a bit."
i said to him,
"i've got a call"

"ok."
he said,
making his way back up the hall
and speaking over his shoulder.

the door shut,
i answered the phone.

"hey you...where are you? how about
taking me to the beach?"

"sure thing."
i said,
"we can have dinner afterwards."

i hung up the phone,
smiled
and stepped beneath the hot shower.

i was glad for the female voices
that still pervade my life,
and for neighbors who spend time
trying to figure it all out...

i'm more stable now
and fortunately the girls just keep on coming.

in the old days,
it was just a little bit different...but not much.

today
i walk
instead of run.

the patterns of aging
are starting their reverse flow
but
my mind still churns forward.

london

Isn't

...and isn't it reality

when you dream
that you are dreaming,

only to discover
that you've never been awake

at all.

chicago

Keep On

life can be

beautiful.

7 days a week,
24 hours a day...anything
can matter just enough to make
it all worth it.

keep on.

keep beautifully
on...

know when something is about to count,

and live it
with all your heart.

London

Folding

it's hard to know
just how many sides there are to the things
we live.

try them all.

if you will only muster the courage.

at home; living room window, chicago

Ghosts in The Room, and Me in The Middle

i could swear
that there are moments

like tonight. sipping a drink
and nibbling chips dipped in salsas
i brought from my mother's house...little ghosts
in the room.

some years ago
i lived over on lincoln and diversey
in a building built
in the early 1900's. there were troublesome
little spirits who'd come and go
at their own will. slipping in and out

between the walls
and upwards through the cracks in the floor.

i'd wake up some nights
to the rumbling
and shivering of the room
as they passed through
from their realm to ours
and back again.

who knows what they wanted.

some nights
they'd shake my dreams. enter in
in a rush,

get up close in my face
and whisper horrible black images
deep in to my mind.

some nights they didn't bother me at all...but rather
chased the cats about the room,
under the dressers,
and over the bed. i had to use plastic cups most of the time
since either the ghosts
or the cats would send glasses reeling and shattering
across the wood floors.

plastic couldn't break. but dammit,
they sure as hell tried to break them.

in time,
we had an agreement. i wouldn't fuck with them
if they wouldn't fuck with me.

the word must have gotten out
because now i know when they show up.

i know they're here.

they must have heard
there was an easy going,
personally distracted,
unintimidated guy
in the middle of the city.

because now they show up...usually
with a friend or two. sometimes more.

but none of us
makes any big deal out of it.

we go on about our business,

and i've asked them to leave my old cats
alone.

"hang out,
sit in the window,
or watch the rain fall,"
i said to them once,
"just don't mess with my old cats...they need their easy rest. aside
from that,
i've got God and Sweet Jesus on my side. and you KNOW what that
means..."

so now
they do just that. take a seat,
stare out the window,
or just plain take up rest and refuge before

being forced by their own demons
back in to the night air.

or perhaps they go back to the graveyard gates
that expelled them in the first place.

so tonight they've arrived once again. slipped in
just as quietly as they sit in the corner widow.

if i could help them
i would. but i know it's probably best
for all of us to stay on our own sides of the fences
that border our worlds.

aside from that,
we still have our agreement. we each
and all
have our own space
in time. this time
or any other.

so on some nights,
like tonight,

with the little ghosts in the room
and me with my drinks, chips, and salsas…

we somehow fit perfectly
in to each other. like
a space-age
mystical
invisible puzzle
that solves itself
when nothing
is altered or disturbed.

in fact
those little ghosts
in the rooms
have taught me little things
over the years.

live and let live. friendly
but firm. know the boundaries.

and most of all,
always be well intentioned

even if you don't plan on giving a damn
at all.

so tonight i say to them:
rest easy,
spirits...those demons that chase you around can't touch you here.
because
just like me,
you've got God and Sweet Jesus on your side. stick around longer
if you have to.

just
please,

don't slam the doors
or windows on your way out. and leave those cats alone!

amen~

surface level; earth

What Are They Thinking

i've sometimes pondered
christ,
ceasar,
ghandi,
hitler,
churchill,
rourke,
reagan...sitting
on their front porch
under a setting sun.

i wonder what they think
or thought of

in their most generously
quiet moments.

i was always amazed,
upon moving to a new place,
getting the previous tenant's mail
now and then. magazine and credit card offers,
birthday cards from long lost friends. once
i even opened an envelope
to find a scribbled note about
getting together some time - how they'd lost touch. no money though...
(which
is what i was secretly hoping for – haha)

sitting over breakfast today,
i discussed life with a friend...the sickening nature of
this cave dwelling mad man - bin laden...UFO's,
the state of things
as they are
and are not.

i love to think about the time before time...and how there has ALWAYS
been something - because there is no time where there could EVER
be nothing. and
how it never ends and never will.

"well before time - back then,
there were only gasses and dust"
my friend said.

"well where the hell did all those gasses and dust come from?"
i laughed,
shaking pepper over my eggs.

eventually we paid the bill and parted.

i crossed lasalle street
near chicago ave.

i wanted to pick up a newspaper
to see what new madness was printed in there.

i was not suprised to read that the world was still upside down,
the gas prices were still up,
and the chicago bulls were still lost somewhere between slow
and stop.

i suppose throughout time,
for some it's happened all too fast
(and for some it's happened all too slow)

for me - it's been a little of both,
but rarely when it counted.

which reminds me,
i heard someone say,
"life is mostly lived at arm's length,
looking the other direction
as we long desperately to get back to bed."

there are many truths to that statement.

and it makes me smile
as i try to figure out a way to get off this planet.

upwards or outwards to some far off star
that will surely save the day.

my old door man
on oak street used to know every call girl

within a 6 block radius. i left that building recently...only to find myself
here.

"i can get you any girl you want"
He'd say..."a Cadillac too. With ALL the papers – 4 grand – CASH."

i'd grin,
laugh,
or both.

sometimes i wonder
if i'm anything like the people
of history. ceasar,
jack the ripper, charlie brown,

or any of the rest of them.

maybe they've found their ways to the stars...one of those twinkling
out there in the night.

i walk to the window to see what i can see. but damn it.

it's monday night.

and it's black and raining
here at 1012pm.

i'll have to take up these thoughts
at some other time.

until then: i watch
out for the humans. you never
know just what's on their mind...sitting in a coffee shop
or behind the wheel of an automobile...

3am at Redno5, Chicago

3am At Redno5

it's hard
to look good at 3am.

after drinking most of the evening
someone
somehow
comes up...

"hey,
let's get a photo of you!"
they yell
over the pounding music
and bouncing bodies.

you muster whatever drunken coherency
you're able,

and smile nice
for the person
as they click,
flash,
and slip back in to the darkness.

back among the mass
of bodies,
bumping and grinding to the things
that bump and grind
at this late night/
early morning hour.

yes,

it's hard to look good at 3am. but at 3am,
after drinking most of the evening,
looking good isn't necessarily
the point.

you're there. it's been a long night. and you look for
signs of decency
as you enjoy the music,
the chatter of friends,

and people you've never seen before.

somehow
someway
you'll make your way home
and forget most of what happened...

of course
then you'll see your photo somewhere
and remember that the night was mostly tolerable,
the music was good,

and the end,
you finally decide,
came way too soon.

when i'm home,
sometimes i wish i was still out there.

not necessarily looking good. but
certainly enjoying every minute of it.

i've always had this strange love
for the night...

I've Been Waiting

and i can't tell
if i'm still
in a far away dream
or
if
i've become awake.

sweet
girl

won't you open your eyes
and tell me what i need to know.

the clock
is just out of reach.

the sun is making its way
through
the window.

the breeze
pushes
itself
through the curtains...

sweet
girl

won't you open your eyes
and show me what i need to feel.

the cats stretch
and yawn
and
the heartbeat
of the street below
begins to beat.

she sleeps there
next to me

or is it a dream...
sweet
girl

won't you open your eyes
and kiss me with your lips
(which
have saved me so many times before)

a taxi cab honks
and a fire truck wails in the distance.

i hear the newspaper delivery man
making his way outside my door...thump
thump
go the morning papers
as he lines our halls with the new day's news.

i can't remember how
i came to be
in this place

or
if it is just a

mixture of exaustion
and hope (it may be just a simple dream…)

sweet
girl

won't you open your eyes
and whisper to me
everything my
ears burn to hear.

i've been lying here for hours,

watching the blackness of night
turn a purplish haze.

and
now the yellow
of early morning is marching across the sky

sweet girl
don't you know,

i've been waiting all night for you
to open those eyes...

i've been waiting.

so wake up and kiss me.

let's forget the world outside
and stay wrapped up for days.

we'll order pizza or chinese,

and just when we think there is nothing left to give,
we'll sleep

then. we'll begin again…

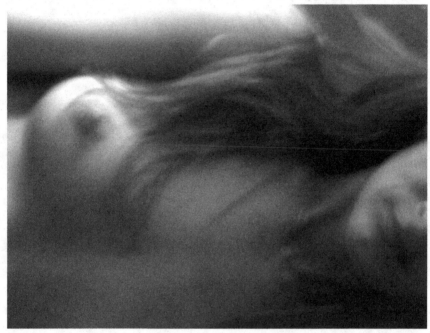

then. we'll begin again.

Dennis

i don't remember his last name
but
i remember his first name was dennis.

he was in my 1ˢᵗ grade class.
strange.
quirky.
and i thought he had some special
sort of secret for the longest time...but like
many things,
i soon realized how wrong i could be
about people.

there are many human injustices
that i will never understand.

well,
dennis was quiet,
smiled a lot,
and his blondish
boyish hair
was always a bit disheveled. he
always seemed a bit nervous.

he never really quite knew the answers
to any of the questions he was asked in class.

in fact
when asked anything,
the smile on his face quickly faded
and
he'd stutter,
saying "um" between the stutters
and would finally say something like

"um,
im not sure...i don't know the answer."

he would sit down
in his seat...disheartened.

no one seemed to like him...not even
the teachers.

and
their disapproving looks
were apparent
even to my young eyes.

i would see the teachers snicker
when he walked past.

i'd always
wait a few seconds for him to pass,
then my eyes would shift to the teachers
standing in the hallway...they'd be whispering
and pointing...sarcastic smiles on their faces.

dennis always wore a rope
around his waist,
carefully threaded
through his "sears toughskin" jean
belt loops.

ms foss,
our 1st grade teacher,
always asked dennis where his
regular belt was.

and to this he'd stand up and respond,
"my mother is washing it today"

i'd see her roll her eyes,
sometimes huffing at his response.

he'd smile nervously,
look around the room to see if anyone
was laughing at him,
and sit down.

even in my little 1st grade mind,
i felt sorry for him,
but admired something about his innocence.

now and then
i'd offer to play with him at recess,

and as soon as we'd start in
my friends would call to me...

"don't play with him! he's likely to take that
rope off and hit us with it!"

i'd say,
"sorry dennis,
i'm going to go over there and play
with those guys...let's play tomorrow or something."

in my own weakness,
i'd leave him standing there
alone.

during class,
at times,
he'd look back to me...over his shoulder.

he'd smile at me,
perhaps thinking that
this would be the day we'd play.

eventually,
i just started looking the other way.

i was beginning to
formulate
adult childishness back then...with
all the judgments that go along with it...

there are so many injustices
which are seemingly out of our control.

they're based
on weaknesses
of the human spirit...fears...

sometimes
kids would pass a note.

'dennis is a sissy!'
it would say...or,
'dennis is dumb!'

i'd crumple it as soon as i had it passed to me,
give the giver of the note
a roll of the eyes
and pass it back

i didn't want to be a part of that inevitable process...not yet.

dennis never really had enough to eat

and when we had hamburger friday (mcdonald's delivery)
he'd always bring a sandwich from home.

on hamburger day,
if you didn't order a mcdonald's hamburger,
you'd have to take your bag lunch
and eat in the gym.

the rest of us whose mothers ordered
hamburgers
got to eat in the class room
and we'd listen to records or play musical chairs before making it
outside for
the lunch recess.

i'd always have my mom order extras
and when i saw that dennis only had a sandwhich,
i'd slip him one while he made his way
to the gym.

as the year progressed
we spoke less and less
and by the time the year
came to an end his mind seemed to have drifted a little too far.

but one afternoon...the last day of the school year,

it was flag day
and we were splitting up on teams
for various foot and bag races.

no one wanted dennis on their team
and he ended up being picked last.

after the races
we all ran over to the tire house
to play our daily rounds of "flush."

a game which karl wendling had made up.

dennis was just hanging around
outside the tire house when
april macies
ran past him and slapped him in the head.

"dennis! dennis! dennis!"
she was yelling.

dennis chased her down
and pulled her to the ground by the hair.

i'd never seen him so valiant...so violent...so
passionate.

the nervous smile was gone.

he screamed
he pounded
he pulled hair...

the teachers ran over
and pulled him off of her
as his arms flailed.

"no justice."
i thought...THIS is the world we live in.

i followed the dusty
mess of teachers and dennis being
dragged in to the class room.

april was crying and kept saying,
"you're in big trouble, dumb dennis!"

i stood quiet as
he stuttered
and "um'd" through
the intense teacher questioning...he cried a bit.

i finally spoke up

"april started it...dennis was just standing
there when she ran past him and slapped him
in the head"

there was a silence

the teachers didn't want to believe
he was innocent...in a way, i think they had some fear of him.

and
even more than that,
they wanted
little blonde april macies
to be as innocent as her pigtailed blonde hair.

she was far from innocent.

"ok - everybody out"
one of the teachers said,
"every one except for april and dennis"

345

i was escorted out
by mr hughes
and i never saw dennis again.

summer vacation came
and we all went our separate directions...

the next year came
and someone said
dennis had moved away.

"they probably sent him to a funny farm!"
april said.

i wondered about him now and then
but
eventually he faded from memory.

by the time 3rd grade started,
we were all firmly placed in
our social classes.

dennis was removed from the scene,
but a new one had taken his place.

doug hansen was his name...new in town. chubby as chubby can get.

and he farted a lot when he bent over...his face always
turned red and kids would say
"there is a green mist coming out of doug's butt!"

that winter he told us that
santa clause and his reindeer
had
left paw prints and sleigh marks on his roof.

he got beat up good for that one.

by this time,
april macies began to become a bit strange too.

she would turn a bottle of
elmers glue upside down and
pour it in to her mouth.

"look what i can do!"
she'd exclaim.

"ooooooooo....grosssssss!!!"
everyone would yell.

she always asked me why my skin
was so dark
and if my parents made me that way.

"does your skin taste like chocolate?"
she'd sarcastically ask.

one afternoon
john pelton put 5 pieces of bubble yum gum
in his mouth,
chewed it in to a mass of goop
and slapped it in to april's hair,
mushing it around deep in to her scalp.

well
april screemed,

john pelton laughed,
and i stood there,
in wonderment...in silence.

i didn't much like
anyone i saw

but i did love to play...

it was about this time
that i found comfort in being alone.

with my bike
i'd ride to imaginary worlds.

with my fingers i'd build imaginary cities in the sand.

with my ears
i'd hear the calls
of the wild jungle

with my feet,
i'd run from imaginary aliens,
over mountains
and through burning houses...

somewhere in the distance
i'd hear my mothers voice
calling to me through the neighborhood.

with the same bike
with the same fingers
with the same ears
with the same feet

i'd come running home
from my imaginary worlds...

just in time for dinner

and out there
now there are
a million of dennis
a million aprils
a million john peltons
a million doug hansens
and
a million teachers

and i still sit here
alone

feeling a little bit sorry for all of us...

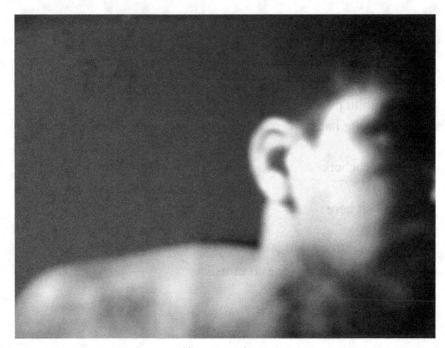

self portrait; chicago

Decent

most people
are relatively decent

to a degree,

as long as you don't look too terribly
close.

it's far better
to glance
than it is to stare (which is why i mostly prefer

photos
to the real thing),

and better to exist
hand in hand
with superficiality,
than to become disillusioned
by a clouded mind
wishing for things to be
just
as they are
imagined.

and despite
their ramblings,
most people are not very interested in you.

aside from what you can offer,
provide,
or get for them in some future
scenario
yet to be played out.

but
they play nice
just like you (or i)
play nice,
and
isn't that just how it is
as you (or i)
do the same...

in a way
it's a shame, though. because

even when we meet that rare,
vulnerable soul,
unhardened by the rest,

we hardly recognize it...or take the time
to see the difference,

causing the inevitable buildup
of indifference
which leads to more of the same...more of the above,
which we sign on the dotted line
somewhere below.

and still,

when the phone rings
or we hear
a knock at the door,
we pick up...open up...and
somehow,
someway,

the way we were
was probably never true at all.

and if i remember my way back
to those things i imagined of myself,

i'll bottle it up
and sell it to anyone
willing to taste something new
and real.

and just the way
we like it when
we want to be a somehow, somewhat decent human being.

even below the superficiality
of our day to day
existence...

somewhere in a remote area of illinois

As Is, To Heaven

somehow
i feel as we
all surely feel. that life will continue
as is,

until the last curtain is drawn...which we somehow envision
will come without warning
and/or without any drawn out
discomfort
or pain.

we'll sail up and down
that river,

taking in the sights,
sounds,
shrieks,
and laughter...planting a kiss
here or there
as we balance our checkbooks
and wink at the creditors
passing by.

every morning
we slowly turn,
stand,
and stretch
our hands
miles in to the sky...sure
that things,
as they are,

will continue.

good
and sometimes bad.

but always just
bearable enough
to keep us comfortably
numb.

the clock ticks.

the sun sets,

then rises again.

and all the while
the moon takes its turn
nibbling at stardust
in the distance.

and somehow
life continues
as it always continues.

as is.

as is.

as
is.

and then suddenly.

STOP.

at least
we hope
it'll
be that simple.

a plane crash would do it for me. no slow,
sleepy,
painful stretches
in the death ward
of some hospital.

i'll take a quick
snap of the neck
and
"as is"

until that very last moment.

in a life
so twisted
and unfair,

it's the least the universe
could offer us
as we make those first steps upon
that one way road
to Heaven.

berkley, CA

Can't Change The Past (but the present was always our future)

even though cammy was the same age
as the rest of us,
she always seemed
so much more mature.

when she managed to make her way out
to where we were,
she never drank much
and never stayed too late. she was always
better dressed
than the usual range of kittens
and cats.

she never engaged in the small talk
that usually dominated the night.

she followed us down to key west one time.

but even there,
she never let it all hang out (as they say),
and never did anything worth remembering. just sipped
her drinks, shopped,
and went home alone
each night.

however,
she DID once let me kiss her at a halloween party. neither
of us was dressed for the occasion,

and we laughed,
sipping our beers
as the parade of drunks
mumbled
and stumbled past us on their way to the bar.

"why don't you ever have anyone?"
i asked her.

"no one asks."
she said.

"really..."

i let the moment sit
for about 3 minutes,

before asking her the obvious...

"well,",
she said,
"ASK!"

"what if i DON'T ask."
i laughed,
"maybe i'm just like the rest of them.".

she sipped her beer,
smiling,

and *suprise*suprise*

quickly slipped her tongue
in to my mouth.

we continued
for a few minutes,
my heart pounding. scared,
even. she was so startlingly pretty
it could be breath-taking when you didn't expect to see her. and
i was always afraid of her
in some strange way.

as if our friendship
relied on us NOT sleeping together. and as we kissed
i realized,
i never really liked her at all. it was
her mystery.
THAT was her power. i suddenly realized
i knew almost nothing
about her. or even where she was from.

i felt uncomfortable afterwards...
"i'm getting another beer,"

i said,
"want one?"

i got us two beers
and later we made our way home.

she asked me in
as we approached her place.

just then
a girl i was sleeping with
happened up.

"what's going on?"
she asked,
"hi CAMMY."
she added,
sarcastically.

we all talked nervously
for a few minutes
when the girl i was sleeping with
finally tugged at me.

"let's go."
she said.

"see you around cammy."
i said,
and made my way home with the girl
i'd soon be rid of.

she refused to sleep with me that night,
only peppering me with questions about

what the hell i was doing walking home
with a 'bitch like cammy'.

"i don't know,"
i said,
"it was nothing."

and it really was.
today,
cammy and i are still the same age,
but it's been years since i've seen her. probably
good we never got together that night. chances
are i'd have fallen madly in love with her
blonde hair and long legs,

only to write her off the day
she passed 25 years...ha ha.

knowing what i know of myself
and my obession
with youth,
i would have been very bad for her. heaving
mountains of passion over her,

only to pull it back
when my desires waned...

because it was
always like that. and yes,

that's just the way
it is.

some of the best roads
are the ones we never took.

so here's
to the present...it was always
my future. it is always
what i was supposed to be.

#76, Chicago

VII.

have you heard the exciting news???

call.
write.
text your friends...

syphilis
is back. and to some,

it must feel like it never left.

ha ha ha. such
a strange, beautiful,
and wonderful world...

walking home at 320am; chicago

Tuesday Night Memo

...so andy's girlfriend of almost 2 years
decided to leave him for a GIRL.

of course
this left him open to
the waterflow of bad advice
which soon followed.

"dude"
someone chimed in,
"the problem is he didn't fuck her hard enough...chick
like that - you have to FUCK HER REALLY GOOD."

i had to laugh
because in my experience:
with the girls that count,
it's not always about the fuck. but the fuck
can fuck things up
when other things are already fucked up.

and so it goes.

in other news,
the chicago cubs are in 1st place. the chicago
white sox are in last place. and someone
somewhere purchased a brand new car
that is sure to break down
in the coming weeks.

it's amazing
to see life unravel
in so many chaotic manners
all at once.

i mean,
priests pray for sunshine
as farmers pray for rain.

and somewhere in the mix,
we're there...relying on the things
that slip so effortlessly
through our fingers.

because with everything
that counts,
they usually get fucked up
when other things related to them
are already fucked up.

can anyone
anywhere
find a more simple and lovely
explanation for that? if so,
do tell.

and if not,
try something different...and also
please refrain from passing
along ridiculously
ridiculous advice.

gracias.

P.S.:
there will be a team building meeting
tomorrow at 1pm,
and we'll be celebrating this month's birthdays
at 430pm. cake
and soda
will be served. PLEASE

be on time.

lincoln park zoo; chicago

Kalidescope

dear friends...i do believe we've forgotten how to wonder.

"why
why
why
why why...and how?"

ha ha...

there came a time
when we stopped asking out loud.

and
internally,
fear
took it's place
at the front of the line.

but
i wonder,

what it would be like

to wonder
just like that

again...

to be able to look
at something
and see the amazing-ness
of it. like we are looking at it
for the first time,

or from a new
and exciting angle
at every moment.

bring back
                that innocence...i plead

and beg
of you. let's look at the world
through a kalidescope.

and remind me
to go flying through my imagination
every time i see a polar bear
fitting perfectly
in to the bluish-blue
sky.

chicago

Roll The Helicopter

...the last time i saw julie
she was engaged,
apparently happy,
and doing well at her new job. banking of some sort.

"you're such
a good guy"
she'd say,
"you have to find someone
like i found my josh"

she was 26,
quite lovely,
and full of that family itch...

"when that screen door slams,"
she once explained,
"you want to know
that someone is home and
waiting for you."

i actually believed
what she said
when she said it,

because she always had that sentimental look
when she talked about life,
love,

and as she always said,
"my josh" whenever she referred to him.

she seemed to be in love with wonder
as she wondered about love...

we lost touch for a few months
but when she called me on a wednesday afternoon,
i knew something must be awry.
"i'm in trouble."
she said.

she had been having get-away lunches
and before bed time drinks
with some guy she'd met while
on the JOB...

"he took me up
in a helicopter ride
over the city."
she cried,
"and as we rode around
he pulled out a ring...what the hell
am i supposed to do???"

"what about that josh
you speak so much of"
i asked.

"oh GOD."
she cried,
"i LOVE josh. i mean i LOVE HIM."

"apparently there's a little room
for this other guy."
i half laughed...not wanting to sound too
harsh.

we search to hear
and say words we never speak...never quite
getting there
unless we're about to lose it all...or when
we gain some poison
we've toyed with
for a little too long.

there are times we learn more
from a 12 week
mistake
than we learn from years
of the best internal advice.

"what are you going to do?"
i asked her over drinks
later that night.

i can't even remember
what she said...it was late when
we got around to talking about it again.

but as i think of her at 957pm,
i send out a message. because
if i could,
i wouldn't want to change her mind...but simply
wish her luck,

with which ever way
the helicopter lands.

josh too...

Contact

it's good to know when
you've got the touch…

because it's far too often we think otherwise. riddled
or frozen
with insecurities which never solve a thing.

i've kissed well over a thousand girls in my life…and did
the things i pleased with nearly every single one of them
as i made my way.

now mind you,
this is no lie…something i'm neither proud
or ashamed of. just simple human math

mixed with little erotic neutrons
and protons,

or little winks in the right
and wrong directions...or upside down
when the moment called for it.

as i grew in to adulthood
i had singers telling me all the things i never
yet knew.

shock the monkey.
thunder road.
little purple love
while drowning in purple rain.

writers told me more...and the adult humans
i knew
had other ideas...

live and learn.
keep the faith.
never go to bed angry
and never wake up late...
i can't say i listened to any of them,

but in many ways i understood
them all.

it's the things we don't know
that keep us shaking hands
and making love
day after night
after night
after day.

nothing seems
to make it for us
aside from contact.

a glance,

hope,

15 minutes of white hot
slippery
ecstasy
which always solves it all (for a while, at least).

before we ever knew
what it was we wanted,

we knew what made us feel safe.

contact.

touch.

doubt appeased and satisfied in a smooth
and spicy way...

so kiss.

kiss.

and do it again.

softly.
deeply.

as lovely
as you ever dreamed a flower to open
in the wide universe stretching out before you.

then,

do it again…once more for luck. or just because
it's what we're meant to do.

because contact is what it's all about.

when i fall to sleep
at night,
i often dream in red. or little
shades of blue…

see the people
walking around you…to the left
and to the right.

contact.

have the touch. touch it. and let it be touched.

one stroke
of a finger
and we're wrapped
between the sheets
like we never,
yet always, imagined…

drive that thunder road,
feel that purple rain…live and learn.

and don't sleep too late
unless it's in the arms
of something
or someone lovely.

because it's that commitment to contact
that
always promised,

but only delivered

after you truly understood...

London

Looking Forward; Looking Back

i sometimes go the places i grew up. i may find myself
back on the streets of the town i grew up in,

and nothing looks the same. there are familiar
corners
or familiar street signs,
but the names of the people i knew there
are fading.

sometimes i remember a first name,
or something we did...or something we said. then it
just
drifts
away.

drifts to some place in the fogs
of my memory,

and i'm suddenly confronted
with

today.

it's amazing. we look down familiar paths
and expect to see the things we always knew. we see
familiar faces
but they're older now. and the things we knew of those faces
have changed in ways we never expected
way back when we lived them for the very first time.

looking forward
or looking back. we never know just what will count
or what will fall by the way side,
never to be known again.

a hello. a kiss. a glance
from a human
we may never know...but could have known just
the same.
that first sip of lemonade. that first august
breeze. or the first time
we heard the word
"no.",

and how it shattered our world.

i'll always remember her face...just before that first
embrace
on that first night. not sure if a kiss was appropriate,

or how long it would be before we fell
in to my bed.

as for another,
i'll always remember the way she'd wipe her mouth afterwards. or
how she'd scream
whenever she was scared. the best reaction she could muster
when confronted by the hardness of life.

the fastest man
does not always win the race. and the most beautiful
girl is never the most happy.

and still,

it's amazing. we look down familiar paths
and expect to see the things we always knew. we see
familiar faces...older now. and strangely different,

because we now see what's on the inside. it has all
drifted, quite appropriately,
to the surface.

and for a brief moment
we look forward as we are looking back. faced
with the ever-present
reality of the now. and see that everything
is really exactly as it seems.

She Came for A Visit

she came for a visit

after 8 long months,
she finally returned

each morning,
each afternoon
and each night
overflowed with
l
o
v
e
.

we twisted and turned each other
in every direction

smiling,
laughing...dancing at
each other's
finger tips.

smiles turned to kisses.

each kiss began a tender embrace

and
each tender embrace led to breathless ecstacy.

each moment of ecstacy
made us ache for more.

having exhausted
every last nerve ending,
we would sleep in each others'
arms for hours.

outside,
sirens blasted as they've always blasted,
birds flew as they've alway flew,
taxi cabs honked as they've always honked.

and
far beneath the ground below
hot embers shifted the plates of the earth.

deep inside me
the quakes
rumbled
and shifted
as
l
o
v
e
danced sweetly overhead.

she flew away today.

a hunk of metal, glass and gasoline
whisking her in to the afternoon sky,
westward
to the breezes of san diego.

i miss her now
as i type these words at
1040pm.

i'll soon make my way to the empty bed
where her scent still lingers.

and
dreams of passion will trickle
in to me
in the middle of the night.

outside my window
the chicago streets below
just keep on beating...

i smile
as i
look forward to seeing her
again.

until next time…

mark40e
mark40e@yahoo.com
thanks for reading…spread
the word.

M~

Follow mark40e:
Instagram: mark40e
Twitter: mark40e

*A special THANK YOU to Tori, who re-lit the fire.

Gracias ~!

Sleepy Where You Stand (?)

the people of the concrete chaos
waltz the streets

unawake (and refusing)

London. New York City. Chicago. San Francisco. Tokyo.

i'll have to admit:

London didn't do it for me. and New York City was full of garbage
but it made me smile just the same.

Chicago is my hometown,

but if San Francisco would have me
i really couldn't say no...

and Miami? Key West? not much left to say...they are places so
obvious
that they become boring to the mind.

Tokyo was a rush. just the way I've liked it. and the others...the others
are a blend of memories and blur.

i was mostly drunk and/or high in Amsterdam,
hungover in Bangkok,
and annoyed in Iceland.

Mexico was relaxing
but too damn hot and bright for the eyes.

San Diego. No.
L.A. No.

Iowa City...haha...ha

Madison Wisconsin. Hmmm...

i liked Louisiana.

the French quarter chewed me up and spit me out...like an old enchilada.
back on to the airplane…back to where i'd come from…

the other day i refused to give a quarter to the smelliest bum
on this stretch of division street

"God blessssshhuuu",
he said,
"and have a nice day."

i now know it's the same
all over the world.

from Portland Oregon to Portland Maine.

from
Ginza to Decatur.

from
Paris to St Louis.

the concrete chaos
gobbles
us
up.

bums
smell the place down.

church moms try
to clean it…to make it ready
for something new.

when we're one place
we're sometimes dreaming of another.

and when we get there
we sometimes dream of the place
from where we came.

our whole life is looking forward
or looking back.

quarters are being passed
from one to the next
for just a little piece of a strange and twisted dream…

the next time you start to make a wish,

don't.

remember your earthling friends
who live buried amongst the steel and rubble.

wake up.

and vow to stay that way.

live in the moment. alive. awake.

and only looking back

when you need to know where you
are.

because even the smelliest,
most annoying places add up to a lifetime just the same.

don't be fooled.

because just like
the quarters: the boredom
the chaos
and the hangovers
add up too.

so set them up
and let's knock them back. we've got nothing but time...

and there's a world of everything just waiting to be lived.

see you in Chicago...

Amen.

Printed in the United States
by Baker & Taylor Publisher Services